"Only a person who has been engaged in interreligious dialogue for so many years and at the deepest level of spirituality as Pierre-François de Béthune can write this kind of book. It is not only full of theological insights and historical information, especially on the past giants and pioneers of interfaith dialogue, but also suffused with profound wisdom, especially on interreligious prayer. I cannot recommend this book enthusiastically enough, for those who are beginning to undertake the journey of being religious interreligiously as well as for seasoned practitioners of interreligious hospitality."

—Peter C. Phan
Ellacuría Chair of Catholic Social Thought
Georgetown University

"The author's experience in daringly crossing the theological and ecclesiastical boarders of his own faith in order to enter into the inner sanctuary of another religion—without intruding impolitely but allowing himself to be welcomed as a humble learner—is an art that the Son of God taught us when he took our flesh in silence and mystery. This Son later received God's visible and audible confirmation of his ministry when he humbled himself before John, the most revered Asian Guru of the time, and became his disciple. This is an aspect of Jesus' life that is seldom witnessed to. Fr. Béthune—whose writings I have always read with spiritual profit, and whose experience as described here is an encouragement to those of us Asians who yearn to be or have already been baptized in the Jordan of Asian religiousness—offers us a valuable theological catechesis on the discipline of dying into and rising from the faith of our neighbors."

—Aloysius Pieris, SJ
Tulana Research Centre, Sri Lanka

D1519357

MONASTIC INTERRELIGIOUS DIALOGUE SERIES

Welcoming Other Religions

A New Dimension of the Christian Faith

Pierre-François de Béthune, OSB

Translated and edited by
William Skudlarek, OSB

Foreword by
Dennis Gira

LITURGICAL PRESS
Collegeville, Minnesota

www.litpress.org

Cover design by Ann Blattner.

This work was originally published in French: A la rencontre des religions : Nouvelles dimensions de la foi © 2015 – BAYARD EDITIONS.

1   2   3   4   5   6   7   8   9

Library of Congress Cataloging-in-Publication Data

Names: Béthune, Pierre-François de, author. | Skudlarek, William, editor.
Title: Welcoming other religions : a new dimension of the Christian faith / Pierre-François de Béthune ; preface by Dennis Gira translated and edited by William Skudlarek.
Other titles: Hospitalité sacrée entre les religions. English
Description: Collegeville, Minnesota : Liturgical Press, [2016]
Identifiers: LCCN 2016007172 | ISBN 9780814646069 (pbk.)
Subjects: LCSH: Catholic Church—Relations. | Christianity and other religions. | Hospitality—Religious aspects—Catholic Church.
Classification: LCC BX1786 .B4713 2016 | DDC 261.2—dc23
LC record available at https://lccn.loc.gov/2016007172

Contents

Foreword

In *Welcoming Other Religions*, Pierre-François de Béthune offers an extended reflection on his personal experience and the experience of other Christians who discovered new dimensions of their own faith when they encountered another spiritual tradition (e.g., Buddhism, Hinduism, Islam . . .). But what kind of "experience" is he speaking of? There can be the experience of those who take up a practice developed by a tradition other than their own in order to better their lives—whatever they might mean by "better their lives." There is also the experience of those who give themselves, heart and soul, to a different religious path and then, with a sense of genuine abandon, are willing to be led to inner realms they could never have imagined on the day they embarked on this new way. The experience of Pierre-François de Béthune and of all those he speaks of is of this second kind, and that is what makes his reflections on interreligious dialogue so significant.

Ever since his baptism almost eighty years ago Pierre-François has been a follower of Christ, the one who calls himself "the Way" (John 14:6). Very early in life—at least by contemporary standards—he determined that for him to follow the Way of Christ meant becoming a monk. He entered the monastery of Saint-André in Bruges, Belgium, and he was sent to Rome to study theology and then to a monastery founded by Saint-André in the Congo. Inspired by the example of Blessed Charles de Foucauld, he thought of remaining in Africa for the rest of his life, but eight years later he returned to Europe, believing that the time had come for Africans to determine their own future. However, his experience of learning an African language and adapting to the local culture played a major role in his decision to do everything he could to help Westerners open their eyes and hearts to other cultures and religions.

On his return to Belgium, he became part of the Benedictine community at Clerlande, near Brussels. Several years later he was elected prior. In the meantime he had made another important discovery. When he returned to Rome for further study, he met a Japanese tea master, Michiko Sōmei Nojiri, who introduced him to the tea ceremony (*chadō*), a spiritual "way" that is so characteristic of Zen Buddhism. His experiential discovery of Buddhism led him to Japan where he was received by Suzuki Sochū Rōshi, the master of Ryūtaku Temple at the foot of Mount Fuji. He was able to spend some time there with the *unsui* (novice monks) and make what might be called a second novitiate. This experience led him to a profound realization that every authentic spiritual path, if followed with dedication, can lead one to amazing discoveries of hitherto unrecognized dimensions of the Christian faith.

As Henri Le Saux did in India, Pierre-François could have remained in Japan and let himself be totally penetrated by this culture that was so profoundly marked by the "way of tea," *chadō*; the "way of the Buddha," *butsudō*; and so many other ways—*shintō*, the "way of the *kami*" (Japanese divinities); *shodō*, the "way of the brush"; *kadō*, "the way of flowers." Once again, he decided to return to his monastery. He recognized the importance of immersing himself in the spiritual quest of his Western contemporaries and of offering them the testimony of a Christian who was resolutely open to the spiritual traditions of other religions. By "resolute openness" I have in mind those Christians who are "prepared to learn and to receive from and through others the positive values of their traditions" and to accept that "the way Christians sometimes understand their religion and practice it may be in need of purification," words taken from "Dialogue and Proclamation: Reflection and Orientations on Interreligious Dialogue and the Proclamation of the Gospel of Jesus Christ."[1]

When he was back in Belgium, Pierre-François became one of the founders of DIMMID, *Dialogue Interreligieux Monastique•*Monastic Interreligious Dialogue,[2] and then its secretary general for twenty-two years. In this capacity he was named a consultor to the Pontifical Council for Interreligious Dialogue, which, along with the Council for the Evangelization of Peoples, produced the above-mentioned document. He also took part in regional organizations for interreligious encounter, especially Voies de l'Orient.[3]

The experience of Pierre-François shows that many of those who engage wholeheartedly in interreligious dialogue feel that they are called to go further, even to the point of allowing themselves to be transformed by what they discover in the

[1] Nos. 49 and 32. The document was published conjointly by the Pontifical Council for Interreligious Dialogue and the Congregation for the Evangelization of Peoples in 1991. Accessible on the website of the Holy See: http://www.vatican.va/roman_curia/pontifical_councils /interelg/documents/rc_pc_interelg_doc_19051991_dialogue-and -proclamatio_en.html.

[2] See its website, www.dimmid.org.

[3] Voies de l'Orient is an independent organization but always in liaison with those responsible for the pastoral ministry of the Catholic Church of Brussels. In May 2014 Voies de l'Orient organized its sixth conference on the theme proposed by Pierre-François de Béthune, namely, interreligious dialogue as a "way of interior transformation" (what Raimon Panikkar called "intra-religious dialogue"). Its final message can be found on its website, http://www.voiesorient.be /?page_id=3653, in French, English, Dutch, Italian, and Spanish.

interior space that has been fashioned by a deep encounter with what is life-giving for their dialogue partners. This is where interreligious dialogue becomes intrareligious dialogue. Those who open themselves to the latter set out on a journey that is both difficult and risky (every such journey is risky!) but also rewarding for those who are sufficiently prepared to enter such unknown and uncharted territory.

The author has come to know this territory well. Taking us by the hand, he gently leads us, showing us routes that are trustworthy and those to be avoided. He begins with the history of the development of the church's attitude toward other religions, mentioning significant events along the way—especially the Second Vatican Council, which showed how important it was to welcome and be in dialogue with the beliefs of others—and also the attempts that have been made to help us better understand what is needed for such dialogue. Convinced as he is that experience is all-important in this area, he introduces us to the life of the great pioneers of religious experience: Henri Le Saux (Swami Abhishik-tānanda), Thomas Merton, Raimon Panikkar (the first to use the expression "intrareligious dialogue"), Christian de Chergé, and a number of others. It is in the light of their experience and of his own long familiarity with the practice of *zazen* and the "way of tea" that Pierre-François speaks to us.

Having introduced us to the pioneers of inter- and intra-religious dialogue, the author embarks on a theological interpretation of their experience and helps us come to a fuller understanding of its meaning for the churches. In the course of this theological reflection, he draws our attention to the dangers of an exclusively intellectual interpretation of the meaning of interreligious dialogue, one that emphasizes the doctrinal differences that separate the traditions involved (Buddhism or Hinduism and Christianity, for example). A solely intellectual interpretation could render suspect and even dangerous the experience of those who engage in dialogue at the level of spirituality. This is the reason the author gives so much weight to the kind of life the pioneers actually led, seeing their lives as a model for authentic inter- and intrareligious dialogue. His reflections on "evangelical hospitality" are especially moving.

In his reflection, Pierre-François does not always make use of technical theological language, but the terminology he does employ is often very biblical. He speaks of "new paths for theology" because, in his view, theology cannot ignore the experience of a growing number of Christians who are open to what is most profound in the experience of the followers of other religious traditions. In this regard, he stresses several aspects of this openness: "a new way of seeing" (the act of being "resolutely open" to others in the sense described above); "a welcoming of poverty" (recognition of the fact that our knowledge of others is very limited and that they can help us deepen our own faith); "an unconditional sharing" (the reciprocity of all sharing at the level of spiritual experience). Making these attitudes, especially "a new way of seeing," one's own is no easy matter, but those who do succeed will discover new ways of thinking about, expressing, and living their Christian faith.

Those who speak or write about interreligious dialogue—and especially about intrareligious dialogue—cannot fail to take into account the witness of those who were intensely involved in it. Because this book does, in fact, take them into account, the reader will here find pertinent reflections on inter- and multireligious prayer, trans-religious meditation, the dialogue of silence, and a *lectio divina* of other religions. Talk of this kind frightens those who are especially concerned about the dangers of relativism and syncretism. However, these are false enemies that can divert us from the real danger, namely, the failure to remember that no expression we give to our experience of God can adequately say who God is *in se*. How we understand the truth of God, the truth of Christ, and the great truths of the faith never completely coincides with these truths. Fearful people do not sense any need for dialogue, but for those of us who do, genuine dialogue, by calling our attention to others and their experience of the Ultimate, allows us to go ever further in our efforts to plumb the depths of Truth. In the end, that is what Pierre-François is talking about, and by doing so, he offers each of us the possibility of entering more fully into the dynamics of the Gospel. He also helps us see that it is not necessary for us to become like the pioneers of dialogue. What is necessary is making our own the humility and courage of these pioneers by opening ourselves completely to others, confident that God is also at work in the heart of their traditions and that each of them has much to say about the mystery that dwells within us.

Dennis Gira
Buddhist scholar,
former Assistant Director of the Institut de science et de
théologie des religions
at the Institut Catholique of Paris,
Member of the international team of Voies de l'Orient

Introduction

The story of the encounter between religions is that of an extraordinary about-face. We have moved from *anathema* to *dialogue*. Such a radical change of mindset has rarely been seen within a community as vast as that of the Christian churches. Over the course of centuries their attitude toward other religions was one of rejection, and now they are disposed to meet them with kindness. What I would like to do here, however, is tell the story of a further evolution by recounting how some Christians have moved from *dialogue* to interreligious *hospitality.* Respectful exchange with a stranger is one thing; it is quite another to welcome the stranger into our home. We take an important step when we engage in cordial dialogue with the followers of another religion, but when we can actually offer hospitality to some of their insights and make them a part of our own spiritual life, our encounter becomes much more decisive. The experience is one that transforms us.

Because it is less well known, this new phase of interreligious encounter calls for study and reflection. Moreover, many Christians who are respectful of other religions wonder just how far their good will should take them. One of the reasons they want to know more about interreligious hospitality is because they are concerned that welcoming certain elements from another religion could pose a risk to their faith.

I will attempt to explore these issues by paying close attention to Christians whose witness to the Gospel involved welcoming another religion and discovering dimensions of their own faith that were hidden. Among these precursors are the monks Abhishiktānanda and Thomas Merton. In the 1950s they commenced a new way of being Christian by taking the evangelical injunction of hospitality with utmost seriousness. They did not set out on this path of spiritual interreligious encounter to satisfy a taste for the exotic. What inspired them, as we shall see, was their desire to offer Christ more space in our ever-expanding world, much as Teilhard de Chardin had sought to do in the field of science.

My intention is not to advance my own ideas but rather to make known the insights of these pioneers, which I have gathered and tried to synthesize over the course of many years. I have had the good fortune to meet many of them and experience the social and religious settings in which they lived. They taught me how to proceed from dialogue to hospitality, making me aware of the risks that are involved and, even more, of how rewarding this evolution can be.

Study of the life of these pioneers also enables us to discover how dialogue at the level of spiritual experience can reveal new dimensions of our own faith. This does not mean adding new articles to the creed! The Christian faith is not quantitative; it does not grow by borrowing doctrines or spiritual methods from other beliefs. However, our faith can develop and become more steadfast by engagement with other traditions. This kind of organic growth is similar to the way a person grows through encounter and friendship. We become more human, more ourselves, through engagement of this kind, and we discover that without such encounters, our latent possibilities would probably never have come to fruition.

A similar development is possible for the faith of Christians when they resolutely welcome believers of another religion or another spirituality. I will go so far as to say that such development has become an essential element of the Christian tradition in our time.

1

The History of a Breakthrough

The Situation Prior to the Mid-Twentieth Century

We are witnessing—and are often participants in—a major development in the Roman Catholic Church. A look at the history of past centuries can help us appreciate the importance of the changes that are taking place and participate in them with greater awareness.

However, let us not become too smug when we contrast our current generous openness to other religions with the narrow-minded intolerance of our predecessors. Lest we become presumptuous, we need only remember that we are still en route. We certainly do understand the necessity of dialogue today, but that does not mean we are all that good at engaging in it! The road is long and we still have miles to go. For centuries we lived with an overriding sense of our own superiority, and that led to haughty disdain for all other religions. Then, in just a few years' time, we did an about-face and began to look on the adherents of other religions with respect. We have gone so far as to invite them to enter into dialogue with us—and then are surprised to find they are not as eager for it as we are. Our temptation at that point is to become indignant at their reluctance, failing to recognize that our resentment is little more than another form of our old attitude of condescension, even contempt! Would it not be more appropriate to express our respect by patience? After rejecting dialogue for nineteen centuries, we have evolved. All well and good. Now, the least we can do is give others the time they need to make their own way, and at their own pace! The question of reciprocity is certainly more complex and I intend to address it later on. What I want to do here is simply call attention to our tendency to revert to old patterns of behavior. We need to make a constant effort to be humble, for humility is the first condition of clear-sightedness in the area of interreligious relations. That is why it is good to recall what our attitude was like in former times, even if it has been somewhat softened during the past century.

To begin with, we can go back to one of the most egregious texts in the history of the Catholic Church. The ecumenical Council of Florence (1442) was nothing less than peremptory when it defined what Christians should believe:

> It firmly believes, professes and preaches that all those who are outside the Catholic Church, not only pagans but also Jews or heretics and schismatics, cannot share in eternal life and will go into the everlasting fire which was prepared for the devil and his angels, unless they are joined to the Catholic Church before the end of their lives; that the unity of the ecclesiastical body is of such importance that only for those who abide in it do the Church's sacraments contribute to salvation and do fasts, almsgiving and other works of piety and practices of the Christian militia produce eternal rewards; and that nobody can be saved, no matter how much he has given away in alms and even if he has shed his blood in the name of Christ [i.e., as a member of another Christian community], unless he has persevered in the bosom and the unity of the Catholic Church.[1]

---

[1] Session 11; February 4, 1442 [Bull of union with the Copts]. Online at https://www.ewtn.com/library/COUNCILS/FLORENCE.HTM.

This conciliar declaration, which expanded on the conviction expressed by St. Fulgence in the sixth century, "Outside the Church there is no salvation,"[2] stood firm until 1949, when it was mitigated by a declaration of the Holy Office condemning the doctrines of Fr. Leonard Feeney of "the Cambridge [in the United States] group," noting that "the principle 'outside the Church no salvation' has not been well understood or examined."[3]

What "no salvation outside the Church" used to mean in practice was that no effort could be spared to convert pagans, because there was absolutely no hope of their being saved by their own religious practice. Eventually, in theological manuals, there was an *excursus* appended to the tract *De vera religione* that dealt with the salvation of infidels and presented a few cases for study. But even at this level the question remained very marginal.

In the area of spirituality, the exclusion of other religions was even more radical. It was unimaginable that a Christian could be guided by any method of asceticism or prayer that was not rooted in the Christian faith. An incident that took place in 1931 at Si-shan, a monastery in China founded by the Belgian abbey of Saint-André, can serve as an example.

> One day, while the monks were on a walk, a Chinese novice and former bonze by the name of Wang, claimed that there were similarities between Buddhist and Christian monasticism. Dom Joliet, the prior, felt that the novice had to make reparation and insisted that he get down on his knees and explicitly declare before his confreres that Christian monasticism was unique. The novice did as he was bidden, but a

---

[2] *De fide, ad Petrum*, 37: PL 65:703.

[3] Letter from the Holy Office to the archbishop of Boston, August 8, 1949. The text of the letter can be found at https://www.catholicculture.org/culture/library/view.cfm?recnum=1467.

couple of days later he again got into an argument and left the monastery soon after.[4]

Daring to see similarities between Buddhist and Christian monasticism was regarded as a form of apostasy; blindness to what they had in common was held up as a monastic virtue.

In time, however, attitudes gradually began to change.

A Turning Point: Vatican II

The declaration *Nostra ætate* was not on the initial agenda of the Second Vatican Council. Not even the Asian bishops had requested a discussion on how to relate to the religions that completely surrounded their Catholic communities. However, during the course of the council it became clear that the church's relation to the great religions of the world needed to be considered. This document, titled "Declaration on the Relation of the Church to Non-Christian Religions," is the shortest of all the conciliar documents, but it has emerged as one of the most significant. It marked a radical change with the past—actually, a 180-degree reversal. However, critics of the declaration were not lacking.

Criticism was first of all directed to the reasons for including such a document in the acts of the council. Some wondered if a certain opportunism might not have been behind the move to speak positively of other religions. According to these critics, as globalization was becoming more and more prevalent, a statement on the church's positive relation to other religions was issued to let the world know that Catholics shared this vision. It was not difficult to answer this criti-

---

[4] Henri-Philippe Delcourt, *Dom Jehan Joliet (1870–1937), Un projet de monachisme bénédictin chinois* (Paris: Cerf, 1988), 209.

cism, which was expressed by the most fundamentalist Catholics. An honest consideration of the motivations of those who drafted this text makes it clear that their intentions were not at all political. On the contrary, they were basically evangelical, as will be apparent in the following chapters.

Another criticism came from the other extreme of the Christian spectrum. Some were concerned that this declaration would have little impact on official theology. In point of fact, it seems that *Nostra ætate* and the experiences of those who actually followed the directives proposed by the document contributed very little to the Declaration *Dominus Iesus*, which was issued by the Congregation for the Doctrine of the Faith in 2000. The reception of a document as innovative as *Nostra ætate* has not always been easy. Openness to other religions has certainly been generous and respect quite sincere, but it has been more difficult to accept all that dialogue implies. There are even some who think that it is not always appropriate to do so.

Thus, in his speech to the cardinals and the Roman Curia on December 22, 2012, Pope Benedict XVI insisted on the importance of interreligious dialogue when he said, "In man's present situation, the dialogue of religions is a necessary condition for peace in the world and it is therefore a duty for Christians as well as other religious communities. . . . [However,] both parties to the dialogue remain consciously within their identity, which the dialogue does not place in question either for themselves or for the other."[5] He nuanced this statement somewhat, but the gist of his thinking was clear: interreligious dialogue must not change the convictions of those who engage in it.

According to this vision of dialogue, *Nostra ætate* did nothing more than propose a change in the way we relate to other

[5] On the website of the Holy See: http://w2.vatican.va/content/benedict-xvi/en/speeches/2012/december/documents/hf_ben-xvi_spe_20121221_auguri-curia.html.

religions. It did not in any way suggest that there should be a change in Christian theology or spirituality.

A statement like that raises a fundamental question: What kind of dialogue is it that excludes, *a priori*, any significant change in those who engage in it? Can we really welcome otherness without being altered? The pioneers of profound interreligious encounter show us very clearly that the acceptance of the possibility of change is a prerequisite for genuine encounter. In fact, the Second Vatican Council opened a door that allows for a major transformation of Christian thought and life. It is this change that I will discuss below.

I should add, however, that dialogue at the level of spiritual experience, which requires a readiness to change, is just one way to engage with other spiritual traditions. In most cases, interreligious encounter takes place at levels other than that of spirituality and normally does not lead to significant changes. What we need to do, therefore, is situate the kind of dialogue that takes place at the level of spiritual experience among the other forms of dialogue. We will then see its specific place and role, which are limited but emblematic.

Four Kinds of Dialogue

In "The Attitude of the Church toward Followers of Other Religions: Reflections and Orientations on Dialogue and Mission," a document published in 1984 by the Secretariat for Non-Christians (currently called Pontifical Council for Interreligious Dialogue), a distinction was made between four types of dialogue.[6] This distinction is illuminating, although it should not be applied too rigidly.

---

[6] Available on line at http://www.cimer.org.au/documents/Dialogue andMission1984.pdf. For some reason, only the Portuguese version is given on the website of the Pontifical Council for Interreligious Dialogue.

1. Peaceful coexistence or the "dialogue of life." The basis of all dialogue is tolerance, which should not be underestimated since it is already a major step toward the possibility of dialogue. It can even become a beautiful expression of respect and esteem. However, at this stage religious issues are not at the forefront.

2. Collaboration for justice and peace or the "dialogue of works." At this stage too religion is not addressed directly. Joint efforts are directed to the social, cultural, or even moral domain. To ensure effective collaboration, any and all religious discrimination must be avoided. Diplomatic dialogue takes place at this level, negotiating agreements that ensure respect for the rights of believers, but religious issues as such are left aside. It should be noted, however, that this type of dialogue leads to the next stage, at least in part, because to work together well, those who collaborate must know one another, even if they avoid speaking of religion directly. Interreligious dialogue should not be limited to this stage, nor to the next, as is too often done when it is said that the aim of dialogue is world peace.

3. Discussion or the "dialogue of experts" is dialogue in the explicit sense of the word. Those involved in dialogue at this level not only try to understand the religions of their dialogue partners but, insofar as possible, strive to arrive at a common understanding, despite the ambiguity of words. The practice of this kind of dialogue often creates strong bonds between those who come together. At the same time, however, they must not let themselves be so fascinated by their study of another religion that they lose the objectivity demanded by this intellectual endeavor. Finally, we note a certain internal contradiction in dialogue at this level. Since the essence of religion is ineffable, an exchange of words can never arrive at what is most central to it. Such dialogue can only deal with penultimate realities. At this level, therefore, interreligious encounter is still incomplete.

4. Complicity or the "dialogue of spiritual experience." This form of dialogue looks for an interior consonance with another spiritual tradition, and even a certain communion with the movement of the spirit in the heart of a follower of another religion.

This fourth form of encounter obviously presupposes the previous three. At the same time, it is also clear that the dialogue of spiritual experience ensures the very possibility of other forms of dialogue. Indeed, if there were not some sense of the sanctity of other religions and of a certain hidden compatibility between all spiritual traditions, no encounter would be possible, because there would be no hope of any real and lasting accomplishment. The dialogue of spiritual experience must be on the horizon of any interreligious encounter. We can even go so far as to say that it is the keystone of dialogue. If the dialogue of spiritual experience is removed, the entire edifice collapses.

A more detailed look at this fourth type of dialogue indicates that "spiritual complicity" is the fullest expression of dialogue. The word "dialogue" is indeed composed of the prefix *dia*, which means "through," and *logos*, "word." Its most literal translation is "through a word." This implies that the word is not solid or overbearing but porous and hospitable. The implication is that words do not cross over an intermediate space that is neutral, but that, coming from the heart, they cut through to the hearts of the dialogue partners.

What we have, therefore, is an "intrareligious dialogue," to use the expression coined by Raimon Panikkar. Dialogue of this kind is not limited to something *between* (*inter*) persons. Rather, dialogue is fully realized *within* (*intra*) persons because it brings about an exchange between my inherited convictions and the discoveries I receive from a witness to another tradition and welcome into my own interiority. We can already see the promise and the risks of such an encounter.

What we must do, therefore, is recall what is required for a spiritual experience of this kind. Without a deep spiritual formation, the risk is great that communion will lead to confusion, fusion, or syncretism, with the result that those who indiscriminately undertake this form of dialogue will become completely disoriented. This concern will accompany us throughout our reflection.

These few details about the dialogue of spiritual experience will suffice for the moment. Seeing how it is put into practice will allow us to be more clear about its challenges and implications.

The Pioneers of the Dialogue of Religious Experience

As we look back, we see that significant developments in the practice of interreligious dialogue were possible thanks to a small number of witnesses who were committed to it precisely because of their faith. By studying the route taken by these pioneers, we will see what perspectives can be opened up by this deepest form of interreligious dialogue.

Let us begin by recalling some individuals: Jules Monchanin (1895–1957), Louis Massignon (1883–1962), Hugo-Maria Lassalle [Enomiya Makibi] (1898–1990), Henri Le Saux [Swami Abhishiktānanda] (1910–1973), Louis [Thomas] Merton (1915–1968), Serge de Laugier de Beaurecueil (1917–1998), Bede Griffiths (1906–1993), Dominique Van Rolleghem (1904–1995), Edmond Pezet (1923–2008), Francis Mahieu [Acharya] (1912–2002), Raimon Panikkar (1918–2010), Vandana Mātāji (1921–2013), Yves Raguin (1912–1998), Cornelis Tholens (1913– 2011), Sara Grant (1922–2002), Christian de Chergé (1937–1996) along with the other monks of Tibhirine. In addition to these figures who are well known because of their writings, there are others, especially those who lived according to the spirit of Charles de Foucauld. They are known only to those who were close to them, but they too contributed to the development of a true intrareligious dialogue. All of them came from similar backgrounds and were marked by the time period in which they were active (between 1950 and 1980; until 1996 for Christian de Chergé). Western students of Eastern religions at that time had relatively easy access to the texts and artistic output of these religions. Think, for example, of Orientalists or Arabists such as Max Müller, Mircea Eliade, Étienne Lamotte, and Louis Massignon, and also of theologians such as Paul Tillich, Henri de Lubac, and Karl Rahner, who began to direct their attention to these religions. Almost all the Christian communities of Asia, on the other hand, remained fairly indifferent, if not hostile, to the great religions around them.

It was in the 1950s, that is to say, before Vatican II, that some Western Christians decided to leave their homeland, not specifically for the purpose of announcing Jesus Christ, but to attempt, in his name, to immerse themselves in a non-Christian milieu. Deeply moved by the example of great Hindu, Buddhist, or Muslim spiritual teachers, they felt the need to do more than simply study them. They decided to abandon their own culture and travel abroad to become, to the degree possible, an Indian with the Indians or an Algerian with the Algerians. Where possible, they even became citizens of their adopted country; Father Jules Monchanin is an outstanding example. He was a renowned theologian in France and used to give conferences about other religions, but in 1939 he decided to live in India and there continue his study and ministry.[7]

These pilgrims had already been devoted to the spiritual life. All of them, in fact, were religious or priests who had received spiritual formation in an institute like the Society of Auxiliaries of the Mission. Unlike other pilgrims and hippies,

---

[7] Françoise Jacquin, *Jules Monchanin, prêtre* (Paris: Cerf, 1996).

who had no particular spiritual preparation, they had already gained great spiritual maturity and therefore could set out with confidence along these unfamiliar ways. Nor were they monks who lived on the margins of their own communities and felt the need to try out something new. They wanted to be obedient to their superiors and remain in communion with them. The living bond they maintained with the church ensured the trustworthiness of their experience. That is the reason their testimony has been widely received in the Christian world.

A final notable feature of these pioneers is the way they evolved. To remain true to their initial motivation, they changed considerably. They never stopped making discoveries and, with their great spiritual freedom, they continuously reviewed their way of relating to other religions. In his journal Father Le Saux regularly notes that he no longer recognizes himself in the books he had written several years earlier and which he is now revising for another edition or a translation.

Immediately after the Second Vatican Council these pioneers were respectfully consulted by the bishops of the dioceses where they resided. Father Le Saux, for example, played an important role in the "All India Seminar" held in Bangalore in 1969.

By the 1980s, in response to the council's encouragement, the local clergy had acquired training in the field of interreligious dialogue. Consequently, these foreign pioneers were no longer so well received. In 1984, Father Edmond Pezet[8] was even asked by his bishop in Thailand to return to France. We can therefore say that the time of the pioneers is clearly demarcated. Nonetheless, it deserves to be studied, because it holds a special place in the history of dialogue, encompassing

---

[8] *Edmond Pezet: A Priest among Buddhist Monks in Thailand* (Brussels: Société des Auxiliaires des Missions, 2012).

the years immediately preceding and following the Second Vatican Council.

Even though, at the beginning of the council, the existence of other religions was not a major concern of the bishops, these pioneers had already made great strides in interreligious dialogue during the previous decade. They were never very numerous, but by their writings, they had a positive influence on the church's reception of the council's teaching in this area. Their experience showed that the openness to other religions expressed in *Nostra ætate* was not simply diplomatic, since an in-depth encounter was both possible and beneficial.

In reality, these pioneers internalized the sea change of Vatican II. They not only achieved a profound intellectual transformation but underwent a true conversion. Every conversion, in the biblical sense of the word, is a discovery of God, as can be seen in the lives St. Augustine, Blaise Pascal, and Blessed Charles de Foucauld. We can say the same thing about Abhishiktānanda or Christian de Chergé. The shock of an encounter with the faith of other believers, Hindu or Muslim, renewed their Christian faith. They were taken aback and challenged when they came into contact with these beautiful spiritual traditions, not merely enriched by them, as they had expected. Their profound encounter with these religious traditions led them to rediscover the Gospel of the Beatitudes.

Reading their writings continues to be timely because they give us not just their ideas but, above all, their experience of discovering new dimensions of their own faith. One might even compare them to the Fathers of the Church, whom we still read today precisely because they devoted their whole lives to searching for the truth for their time. These "Fathers of the Church in dialogue" paid the price that was needed to show that the word of the Gospel is a word that also speaks to and supports the work of dialogue.

Two Emblematic Figures

Two individuals made especially remarkable contributions to the evolution of dialogue. What follows will not be a complete account of the work of these pioneers, but rather will indicate how their interreligious encounters became an intrareligious dialogue that transformed the way they lived out their faith.

Henri Le Saux—Abhishiktānanda (1910–1973)

Father Le Saux deserves special study because in his own life he dealt with most of the ideals and difficulties the other pioneers had to face.[9] He is well known through his many books, including four that are autobiographical.[10] Moreover, since his experience is emblematic, he has been and continues to be the subject of numerous studies.

Henri Le Saux was thirty-eight when he left France for India. He had already been a monk for twenty-one years at Kergonan, a Benedictine monastery in his native Brittany. Those years of formation and maturation were decisive for the rest of his life. Moreover, during his studies he acquired a taste for theological reflection that stayed with him throughout his life. He never renounced his membership in the Benedictine monastic tradition, even when he lived as a wandering *sannyāsi* (a gyrovague!) thousands of miles from his monastery.

---

[9] Shirley Du Boulay, *The Cave of the Heart: The Life of Swami Abhishiktānanda* (Maryknoll, NY: Orbis Books, 2006).

[10] *Une messe aux sources du Gange* (Paris: Seuil, 1967); *Guru and Disciple: An Encounter with Sri Gnanananda, a Contemporary Spiritual Master* (Chennai: Samata Books, 2012); *Souvenirs d'Arunâchala (Paris: Épi, 1978); Ascent to the Depth of the Heart: The Spiritual Diary (1948–1973) of Swami. Abhishiktānanda* (Delhi: ISPCK, 1998).

His fascination with India had already begun in 1934, so he had to show great patience to fulfill a dream that seemed very strange to those around him. But thanks to a contact he made with Father Monchanin, he was finally able to leave for India in 1948, never to return. He lived there for twenty-five years, becoming an Indian citizen in 1960.

On arrival, he proposed to found a Benedictine monastery that would be receptive to Indian culture. He wanted to enrich the centuries-old Benedictine tradition by situating it in a new cultural framework. More broadly, he wanted to prepare the way for "the leaven of the Gospel to permeate the rich dough of Indian monasticism."[11] On July 11, 1950, the feast of St. Benedict, Father Monchanin and he inaugurated the Saccidānanda Kulitalai ashram on the banks of the Kaveri River in Tamil Nadu. To publicize this project, they wrote a book titled *Ermites du Saccidânanda* (*Hermits of Saccidānanda*), which appeared in 1956.

By that time, however, Father Le Saux, who had taken the Indian name of Abhishiktānanda, no longer believed in this project! Moreover, no serious Indian candidate came forward to join this community. In the meantime, he had discovered a much deeper dimension of Hinduism: the ideal of *advaita*, non-duality. His meeting with the great sage Rāmana Maharshi had not only fascinated but deeply shaken him. He asked for some time to reside in the caves of Mount Arunachala, where the sage lived. During several stays at this mountain, between 1952 and 1956, he had a religious experience so profound that it called into question his understanding of his faith, while at the same time strengthening him in his commitment to the Gospel.

---

[11] Jacques Winandy, "Introduction," in Jules Monchanin and Henri La Saux, *Ermites du Saccidânanda* (Paris: Casterman, 1956), 14.

When he returned to Shantivanam (another name for the Saccidānanda ashram), his conversations with Father Monchanin made it clear that their approaches to Hinduism differed considerably. While Father Monchanin was always struck by the gulf that separated Hinduism and Christianity and that seemed to render illusory the possibility of any in-depth rapprochement, Abhishiktānanda always saw that it was precisely in this abyss that one could discover the God who was beyond all formulations, whether those be of Hin-duism or of Christianity.

But this inner evolution was not without a great inner con-flict. We must not forget that this was ten years before the Second Vatican Council, a time when a heavy cloud of sus-picion hung over any theological or pastoral research, as individuals such as the theologians Yves Congar and Henri de Lubac, along with the worker priests, knew only too well. Moreover, the very traditional theological education that Le Saux received at Kergonan provided little help in resolving his dilemmas! Prayer alone allowed him to keep his eyes open to the whole of reality, without giving in to fear.

The discovery of his diary, published in 1986, thirteen years after his death, revealed how intense this intrareligious dia-logue had been. Until then, his books, which were published for the general public with the *imprimatur*, explained the issue well, while also offering some indication of what would be involved in a response to the theological questions raised by the encounter of religions. Abhishiktānanda's diary, pub-lished under the title *Ascent to the Depth of the Heart*, finally let us see at what price those responses, always provisional, had been obtained. One can compare the publication of this very personal diary to the publication of the letters of Mother Teresa to her confessor. In both cases we see how much inner suffering was hidden behind a serene countenance.

By 1952 Abhishiktānanda was able to put his finger on the problem when he said, "India's contribution will above all show itself in what seems most to distance it from Christianity."[12]

> The abyss between India and Christianity is also something fundamental. It is less to be sought in superficial differences, which are, after all, linked with remarkable similarities that are equally superficial. But rather in this: Hinduism is fulfilled in transcending itself, in orienting the best of its adepts toward what is beyond its formulations and rites, in which alone the Supreme Truth resides. For Christianity, the only thing that is beyond understanding is Faith; and Faith is an intellectual adherence. The Christian is not authorized to plunge into darkness.[13]

Therefore,

> How can we believe in the absoluteness of a dogmatic formula? of a rite? hence, of a Church? Could God then be shut up in what is created? . . . Why should not the Word, incarnate in flesh in Nazareth, be incarnate at least in "word" elsewhere? . . . Why should the Incarnation in Galilee be the summit of humanity?[14]

He concluded, "I remain a Christian so long as I have not penetrated into the 'Darkness'—supposing that someday I penetrate that far."[15]

Abhishiktānanda's diary also allows us to glimpse the agonizing struggle he had to undergo to make his way along this path of faith, "From now on I have tasted too much of *advaita* to be able to recover the 'Gregorian' peace of a Christian monk. Long ago I tasted too much of that 'Gregorian' peace not to be anguished in the midst of my *advaita*."[16]

---

[12] Le Saux, *Ascent*, 39.
[13] Ibid., 88.
[14] Ibid., 62f.
[15] Ibid., 89.
[16] Ibid., 74.

March 21, 1956.

Seventh feast of St. Benedict at Shantivanam. A painful one this year. . . .

Since my return [from the Sri Gñānānanda Tapovanam Ashram] anguish has returned. And the very good physical form in which I was when I came back, which was noted by everyone here, all of a sudden gone. Peace and joy for me are there where I am not allowed to go; and yet it is only there that I have enjoyed them with a fullness never found elsewhere. I can no longer live as a Christian monk here; and I cannot live as a Hindu monk. May the Lord take pity on me and cut short my life! I cannot take any more.[17]

At other times, however, he sees the possibility of resolving this tension,

It seems to me I could readily describe my present condition since Arunachala as a dawn, *arunodaya*: even before the sun rises, the sky is lit up. *Jyoti, śānti, ānanda*. The birds are already singing, and my heart is already singing. Await with joy the appearance of the wonderful orb.[18]

After 1956 it seems that his anguish subsides, even though the tension remains. Recognizing that his thinking has already greatly changed since his arrival in India eight years previously, he now resolves to be less trenchant in expressing his theological position.

His meeting with Raimon Panikkar in 1957 allows him to put all his questions in a broader context.

The gospel is not another philosophy It is the proclamation of an event.[19]

The metanoia [repentance, conversion] preached by Jesus is not a transfer from one *dharma* to another. It is a total turning

[17] Ibid., 147f.
[18] Ibid., 147.
[19] Ibid., 298.

round that amounts to nothing less than reaching the stage of "realization."[20]

Jesus is not made greater by refusing to others that which gives him his own glory.[21]

In the last years of his life—he had barely reached sixty years—he was able to transmit the fruit of his experience to some disciples, especially Marc Chaduc (Swami Ajatānanda). On June 30, 1973, he wrote in his journal, "This morning Marc's *dīkshā* [initiation to the monastic life] in the Ganges at 7:30 with Chidanandaji and Krishnanandaji. It was too beautiful—too powerful. The sign has recovered all its value. . . . The four 'celebrants' were simply radiant."[22] A few days later he suffered a heart attack in Rishikesh. He died on December 7, 1973.

The great desire that had called him to India was fulfilled in a way that he could not have imagined, but he could say with the psalmist, "I run the way of your commandments, for you enlarge my understanding" (Ps 119:32). "Fidelity to Christianity; a heart opened to the dimensions of the mystery of India."[23]

Thomas Merton (1915–1968)

The story of the Trappist monk Thomas Merton is very different from that of the other "pioneers."[24] He spent less than two months in Asia! Yet he also made a crucial contribution to the opening of the Christian tradition to Asian spirituality.

[20] Ibid., 299. Brackets in the original.

[21] Ibid., 364.

[22] Ibid., 382.

[23] Marie-Madeleine Davy, *Henri Le Saux Swami Abhishiktānanda, le Passeur entre deux rives* (Paris: Cerf, 1981), 193.

[24] Gilles Farcet, *Un trappiste face à l'Orient* (Paris: Albin Michel, 1990).

He also is well known through his numerous writings, which make it possible for us to have a clear understanding of how he evolved. During the twenty-seven years of his monastic life, he remained in his monastery or in his nearby hermitage, but intellectually and spiritually he travelled far.

When he entered the Trappist monastery of Our Lady of Gethsemani in 1941, he had already undergone a significant interior transformation. He was intensely involved in the intellectual, artistic, and political life of the United States. After entering the monastery, even though he was now a cloistered monk, he remained in contact with this vibrant milieu and even deeply influenced it through his writings, especially during the time of the Vietnam War.

From his early years in Gethsemani, he was concerned about the future of the contemplative and monastic tradition. Initially, he was inspired by the charism of the first Cistercian Fathers of the twelfth century and wrote a few books to make known the vitality of their spiritual quest. He then wanted to expand his view by studying the first Christian monks, the Desert Fathers of the fifth and sixth centuries. Later still, he discovered Zhuangzi and the Taoists. Finally, he was fascinated by the tradition of Chinese Ch'an and Japanese Zen. The trajectory of his evolution is remarkable. Father Louis, as he was called at the monastery, underwent a slow but continuous conversion to a fuller living out of his Christian contemplative vocation.

He never thought of going to Asia to live there as a Zen monk and to be known by another name. He did not experience the anguish of being torn between two traditions, but he did undergo a complete transformation. In his youth, he regarded with amusement his college comrades who were enchanted by the East. Later in life, the discoveries he made, mainly through books, but sometimes also through direct contact with such people as Daisetz Teitaro Suzuki or Thich Nhat Hanh, gradually introduced him to a broader spiritual universe.

He also left a journal, written from 1939 to 1968 and published after his death in seven volumes. The one that is of special interest to us here is the last, which he wrote during his trip to Asia.[25]

He had been invited to participate in a monastic conference in Thailand, and this made it possible for him to organize a trip in Asia that began in October 1968 and was to last a few months. He expected much, and the trip was indeed decisive for him. On his return, he would certainly have written important books on his discoveries. All we have, however, are a few journal entries.

On the first page, written as the plane was taking off from San Francisco, he wrote, "I am going home, to the home where I have never been in this body."[26] He had a sense that this direct encounter with Asia would confirm his intuitions and seal a vital link with Hindu and Buddhist traditions. He felt that beyond an already fruitful *communication*, he could experience a *communion* between the traditions of East and West. In preparation for a lecture he was to give at a conference organized by the "Temple of Understanding" in Kolkata, he wrote,

> I left my monastery to come here not as an academic or even as a writer (it turns out that I am both). I speak as a Western monk who is pre-eminently concerned with his own monastic calling and dedication. . . . I come [as] a pilgrim who is anxious to obtain not just information, not just "facts" about other monastic traditions, but to drink from ancient sources of monastic vision and experience. I seek not only to learn more (quantitatively) about religion and about monastic life, but to become a better and more enlightened monk (qualitatively) myself. . . . I think that we have now reached a

---

[25] *The Asian Journal of Thomas Merton*, ed. Patrick Hart and James Laughlin (New York: New Directions, 1973).
[26] Ibid., 5.

stage of (long overdue) religious maturity at which it may
be possible for someone to remain perfectly faithful to a
Christian and Western monastic commitment, and yet learn
in depth from, say, a Buddhist or Hindu discipline or experience. I believe that some of us need to do this in order to
improve the quality of our own monastic life.[27]

He was able to meet some prominent Buddhists, like the
Dalai Lama, Chatral Rinpoche, and Chögyam Trungpa Rinpoche. During his visit to Sri Lanka in early December, he was
able to visit the Gal Vihara in Polonnaruwa. There, before the
large reclining Buddha, he recounts what he experienced.

I was suddenly, almost forcibly, jerked clean out of the ha-
bitual, half-tied vision of things, and an inner clearness,
clarity, as if exploding from the rocks themselves, became
evident and obvious. The queer *evidence* of the reclining
figure, the smile, the sad smile of Ananda standing with
arms folded. . . . The thing about all this is that there is no
puzzle, no problem, and really no "mystery." All problems
are resolved and everything is clear, simply because what
matters is clear. The rock, all matter, all life, is charged with
dharmakaya . . . everything is emptiness and everything is
compassion. I don't know when in my life I have ever had
such a sense of beauty and spiritual validity running together in one aesthetic illumination. Surely with Mahabali-
puram and Polonnaruwa my Asian pilgrimage has become
clear and purified itself. I mean, I know and have found
what I was obscurely looking for.[28]

It seems clear that Merton had a profound Buddhist experience.

His accidental death in Bangkok on December 10, 1968,
when he was fifty-three years old, made him even more

[27] Ibid., 312f.
[28] Ibid., 233–36.

well-known and emphasized his commitment to the encounter of religions. We especially recall some improvised words of his when he was at the symposium in Kolkata and which were recorded and published in his *Asian Journal*:

> And the deepest level of communication is not communication, but communion. It is wordless. It is beyond words, and it is beyond speech, and it is beyond concept. Not that we discover a new unity. We discover an older unity. My dear brothers, we are already one. But we imagine that we are not. And what we have to recover is our original unity. What we have to be is what we are.[29]

Thomas Merton is at the origin of this desire to recover our original unity, a desire that was then shared by many monks and nuns in intermonastic meetings organized a few years later. The brutal interruption of his pilgrimage did not give him the time he needed to reflect deeply on the experiences he had had. The journal entries he made in Asia evoke the many ways he resonated with Buddhist teaching and experience, their meeting of minds, but he never says how his Christian faith was changed by these decisive encounters.

These two monks and a number of other "pioneers," whom we will also consider, traveled unknown paths, but in retrospect we can see that their explorations were prophetic.

In the light of Vatican II, Christians have understood that the plurality of religions was a "sign of the times," and not a manifestation of the devil, who, as the enemy in the parable, goes about sowing weeds in the wheat fields. Christians therefore have sought to come to a better understanding of these religions and to collaborate with them for the good of humanity. They realized that dialogue was necessary; it was even a duty.

---

[29] Ibid., 308.

Some people went even further, understanding that the encounter of religions could also be a providential opportunity to rediscover and finally develop certain aspects of the Gospel. The change of heart encouraged by the council implies more than a change of ideas; it can also be the opportunity for a new way of living the Gospel.

Ultimately, we see that the history of interreligious dialogue is not linear. The council did not inaugurate a gradual raising of consciousness. While it was only in the 1960s that some finally became aware of the grounds for respecting other religions and collaborating with them, others had already begun to appreciate the place of other religions in the plan of God for the world, and the grace that could come to Christians by interacting with those religions.

For that to happen, these pioneers, as we have seen, had to depart on a kind of exodus. But it was not a headlong flight, a way of escaping from their own tradition, which had become monotonous and bloodless. They were not desperate about their own religious tradition, but they understood that they had to liberate it from a certain fortress mentality in which it had taken refuge. The Catholicism of much of nineteenth- and early twentieth-century Europe was stuck in nostalgia, and the monasticism that was revived after the French Revolution, both Benedictine and Trappist, was essentially a neo-Gothic form of monasticism. Those who restored Western monasticism in the nineteenth century wanted to make it a conservatory of ancient rituals and customs, isolated from contemporary currents of thought. In contrast to this concern for self-sufficiency, the pioneers of interreligious encounter proclaimed that openness and hospitality were the privileged paths of renewal.

Thomas Merton, always attentive to the deepest aspirations of his time, clearly understood the need to get out of a world that was closed in on itself and self-referential. He sensed that one way to accomplish this was through openness to the unexpected grace of Asian spiritual paths, which were so different and yet so similar.

Swami Abhishiktānanda, meanwhile, found at the heart of his monastic vocation the intuition that has sustained monks for at least twenty-five centuries, as expressed in the Vedas, particularly in the famous hymn of the Rig Veda:

> He with the long loose locks supports Agni, and moisture, heaven, and earth:
>
> He is all sky to look upon: he with long hair is called this light.
>
> The Munis, girdled with the wind, wear garments soiled of yellow hue. . . .
>
> You therefore, mortal men, behold our natural bodies and no more.
>
> The Muni, made associate in the holy work of every God,
>
> Looking upon all varied forms flies through the region of the air. [30]

But it is not enough to move easily from the West to the East. What these monks and other Christian pioneers who came from the West to "drink from the ancient sources of wisdom" discovered above all was the action of the Spirit in the sages they met and in the challenge they hurled at the Christian tradition. Their example, which is now well known, inspired many vocations, especially among Christian monks and nuns. It may seem surprising that these people so devoted to silence had a particular skill for dialogue, and yet, thanks to their special attention to the most essential spiritual realities, they made a significant contribution to interreligious dialogue.[31] They were encouraged to do so, in 1974, by the

---

[30] Rig Veda, 10.136.

[31] Bernard de Give, *Un trappiste à la rencontre des moines du Tibet* (Paris: Les Indes savantes, 2010); Pierre Massein, *Un moine chrétien rencontre*

then-president of the Secretariat for Non-Christians, Cardinal Sergio Pignedoli, who noted that "the presence of monasticism in the Catholic Church is already a bridge to all religions. If we tried to approach Hinduism and Buddhism without monasticism, we would hardly be considered religious."[32] In response, Catholic monks created commissions for monastic interreligious dialogue.[33]

In Europe, these commissions gave particular attention to organizing "spiritual exchanges" between Japanese Buddhist monks and European Christian monks in their respective monasteries.[34] During these exchanges, it soon became clear that they could not limit themselves to comparing their monastic customs or the spiritual methods of each tradition. For the Christian participants, fundamental questions arose about the foundations of their faith. In their own place, and with their own charism, monks and nuns entered the ranks of those who are trying to develop a theological approach to these key issues.

It is, therefore, necessary to study the theological implications of these interreligious encounters.

des moines bouddhistes (Dijon: L'échelle de Jacob, 2012); Basil Pennington, *Monastic Journey to India* (New York: Seabury Press, 1982).

[32] *Bulletin de l'AIM* 17 (1974): 62.

[33] Fabrice Blée, *The Third Desert*, trans. William Skudlarek (Collegeville, MN: Liturgical Press, 2011). See the website of Monastic Interreligious Dialogue: www.dimmid.org.

[34] Benoît Billot describes such an exchange in his book *Voyage dans les monastères zen* (Paris: Desclée de Brouwer, 1987).

2

Theological Interpretation

Recent years have seen the publication of numerous theological works about other religions and specifically about interreligious dialogue. In addition to the official documents of the Catholic Church and the World Council of Churches, many other studies have appeared. We can only rejoice to see that this area is finally taken seriously and not simply tacked on to theological treatises as a postscript. We note, in fact, that the questions raised by the recognition of other religions ultimately affect every area of theology, from the history of salvation to eschatology, and have significant implications for our understanding of soteriology and spiritual theology, to mention only the areas that receive the most attention.

However, the current situation of theological development is also troubling, because it tends to go in all directions and even leads to conflicting or contradictory conclusions. However, this is not the place to make an inventory of the many theological treatises created in response to the encounter of religions.[1] What we do need to do is consider the possibility

---

[1] See Paul Knitter, *Introducing Theologies of Religions* (New York: Orbis Books, 2002), for a helpful presentation of the complex status of the theology of religions.

that interreligious encounter may cause further rifts within the church. What can we do to avoid this risk?

Theological Reflection and Spiritual Experience

Sometimes these different understandings are the result of underlying and inconsistent ideologies, but not always. The main problem, I think, is that so many of these theological reflections are not based on *bona fide* experience. Reflection always runs the risk of becoming vapid or ideological when it is not supported by experience, especially in a field as new as interreligious dialogue.

Theology does not start from some fundamental elements of revelation and then develop by deduction alone. It has to be in dialogue with the lives of our contemporaries. This is particularly evident when it comes to interreligious dialogue. Theology is built on and develops with the experience of the faithful.

But not with just any experience. Without a doubt, all experiences have meaning, but in the delicate field of interreligious encounter especially, they are only fruitful when interiorized. Like grapes that have to go through a major transformation to become a good wine, these spiritual experiences have to be subjected to what might be called the alchemy of prayer if they are to be suitable components of good theology. Here, more than ever, the saying of Evagrius of Pontus proves true: "If you are a theologian, you truly pray. If you truly pray, you are a theologian."[2] That is why it is so important to question those who are spiritually engaged in such an encounter.

Among those who have contributed most to the development of the theology of interreligious encounter, we single out two: Raimon Panikkar and Serge Beaurecueil.

---

[2] On Prayer 60.

Raimon Panikkar (1918–2010)

In a work as brief as this, it is not possible to summarize Panikkar's theology of interreligious encounter without distorting it. His understanding of it is complex, and it evolved over his long life.

I will therefore focus on only one of the features of his long and rich life—the evolution of his thought. All the "pioneers" experienced an exodus from their own culture and theology, but he experienced it even more radically.

Raised in a very Catholic environment, he gradually came to an extraordinarily open view of religion that surprised even some theologians. He used to say—intending his words to be at least somewhat provocative—"I began as a Christian, then discovered I was a Hindu, and finally found myself a Buddhist without ever having ceased to be a Christian."

Panikkar was born in Barcelona to a Catholic mother and a Hindu father, but a natural predisposition to intercultural encounter was not something he was especially aware of in his youth. In 1936, at the age of eighteen, he had to flee because his family was threatened by the revolutionaries who had invaded Barcelona. When he returned in the summer of 1939, he was appalled by the atrocities of the Spanish Civil War (it left a half million dead), and in particular by the number of priests and religious who had been killed. In the climate of a Catholicism that had become very vocal and militant, he was attracted to the movement known as Opus Dei, which was in full flower. He entered that secular institute in February 1940, made religious vows, especially that of obedience, and was accepted as a candidate for ordination to the priesthood.

His superiors did not always appreciate the way his thinking evolved and the influence he exercised over his students. For this reason he was obliged to move frequently—from Madrid to Salamanca, then to Rome and Milan. Finally, he was sent to India in 1954, the year his father died.

This first sojourn finally allowed him (at thirty-six years of age!) to become conscious of his Indian roots. He traveled extensively throughout the country and was able to meet some of the protagonists of dialogue, especially Fathers Monchanin, Le Saux, and Griffiths, who greatly impressed him. He saw in them Christians who were not content simply to study Hinduism and to reflect on a theology of religions. Rather, they were resolutely engaged in a spiritual quest at the heart of the Hindu tradition. Thanks to his academic training, he provided them a solid theological framework. In exchange, he received the witness of their spiritual experience. Maciej Bielawski, in his biography of Panikkar, wrote, "Without Monchanin, Le Saux and Griffiths, Panikkar would not only be incomprehensible; he probably would never have become what he in fact became. Without Panikkar, the great threesome of Shantivanam would have turned out differently, and certainly would have been regarded differently."[3]

Later on, during another stay in India in 1964, Panikkar and Le Saux spent time together in a monastic hut in Uttarkashi, at the foot of the Himalayas, where they were able to reflect together about their problematic religious situations. Le Saux was torn between his commitment to the Benedictine tradition and his attraction to *advaita*; Panikkar was finding it harder and harder to accept the directives he was given by his Opus Dei superiors. Together they celebrated a "Mass at the sources of the Ganges," the title of a little book written by Le Saux. [4] Soon thereafter, Panikkar had a conversation with Monsignor Escrivá de Balaguer and definitively left Opus Dei.

---

[3] Maciej Bielawski, *Panikkar, un uomo e il suo pensiero* (Rome: Campo dei Fiori, 2013), 92.

[4] Henri Le Saux (Swami Abhishiktānanda), *Une messe aux sources du Gange* (Paris: Seuil, 1967).

Having made this decision, he then asserted,

> I am a Hindu, and I am proud of it. My father was Hindu, and with his blood he passed on to me the inheritance of the saints and prophets of Bharat [India]. Baptism does not make me deny my Hindu lineage any more than it made Paul, Peter or John deny their Jewish ancestry. India and its scriptures are part of the immense cosmic Testament which preceded the Sinai covenant.[5]

It was also during this period that Panikkar discovered Buddhism and began writing a book that he would return to over the next thirty years: *The Silence of the Buddha: An Introduction to Religious Atheism.*[6] Situating his study of the age-old religion of Buddhism within the study of atheism, the fundamental problem of our time, is typical of his commitment to the spiritual future of humanity. He is not interested in pure erudition—though his writings are very erudite. He always ties his research to the most basic concerns of his contemporaries. This book, some of which is profoundly scholarly, is also an autobiography recounting his own discovery of freedom.

His personal evolution is inseparable from his intrareligious dialogue. In a book that he consecrated to this subject, he explains his thinking:

> Genuine encounter between religions is itself religious. It takes place in the heart of human persons who are searching for their own path. That's when dialogue becomes intra-religious. . . . Intra-religious dialogue is an internal dialogue in which we struggle with the angel, the *daimon*, and

---

[5] Ibid., 58.

[6] Raimon Panikkar, *Le silence du Bouddha. Une introduction à l'athéisme religieux* (Arles: Actes Sud, 2006). When the book was translated into English, its title became *The Silence of God: The Answer of the Buddha* (Maryknoll, NY: Orbis Books, 1989).

with ourselves. . . . In this dialogue, we are in search of our
own salvation, but we allow ourselves to be taught by the
other, and not only by our own clan. . . . Intra-religious
dialogue is, by its very nature, an act of assimilation—one
that I would call eucharistic.[7]

One could cite dozens of pages that describe this process,
but Panikkar's life itself better illustrates his commitment to
this path of interreligious hospitality. Those who had the
chance to meet him personally at his home in Tavertet, Cata-
lonia, during the last years of his long life can attest to this. His
life was the full realization of his ideal of the priesthood, which
he understood as an introduction to *communicatio in sacris*, an
encounter with the God who is beyond all naming.

I have evoked the figure of Raimon Panikkar as an introduction to a reflection on the theology of interreligious encounter because he is a privileged witness to this particular
theological development, which is, perhaps, the most radical
of the changes that came about through the Second Vatican
Council. What pushes theology forward today is precisely
this resolute commitment to an experience of encounter, a
philosophical, theological, and especially spiritual engagement with another tradition.

To better appreciate this change in perspective, it is in-
structive to go back a few years and recall the *modus proce-
dendi* of traditional theology until the mid-twentieth century.
The propositions of Vincent of Lerins (d. 450) are a good

---

[7] Raimon Panikkar, *Le dialogue intrareligieux* (Paris: Aubier, 1985), 8–10.
The passage appears somewhat differently in the English translation:
"The dialogue of which I speak emerges not as a mere academic device
or an intellectual amusement, but a spiritual matter of the first rank, a
religious act that itself engages faith, hope and love. Dialogue is not
bare methodology, but an essential part of the religious act par excel-
lence: loving God above all things and one's neighbor as oneself" (*The
Intrareligious Dialogue* [New York: Paulist Press, 1978], 10).

example, because they were still used to support certain canons of the First Vatican Council. This holy monk of Lérins was certainly pleased to see Christian doctrine develop, but he saw this development as growth in the same way a human body grows. An adult is very different from the child he was, but he remains fundamentally the same person. St. Vincent stated,

> In like manner, it behooves Christian doctrine to follow the same laws of progress, so as to be consolidated by years, enlarged by time, refined by age, and yet, withal, to continue uncorrupt and unadulterate, complete and perfect in all the measurement of its parts, and, so to speak, in all its proper members and senses, admitting no change, no waste of its distinctive property, no variation in its limits.[8]

This comparison with the body, however, is very inadequate. We are now much more aware of another aspect of growth. We know that the integral development of the child depends not only on his or her own potential but also on the child's relations with other people. The same holds true for theology. It cannot develop in isolation, nor is it sustained by its own resources. What makes it develop are the questions and challenges that confront it.

As the opening of the Second Vatican Council drew near, Pope John XXIII began to reflect on the "signs of the times," such as socialization, the emancipation of colonized peoples, the advancement of the working classes, the entry of women into public life. He intuited that the inclusion of these historical realities external to the church were decisive for its future. The response to all these "signs of the times" must first of all be practical and effective, but it also has implications for the development of theology. Even though little was said about

---

[8] Vincent of Lérins, *Commonitorium* 23. PL 50:668. English translation online at http://www.newadvent.org/fathers/3506.htm.

it at the beginning of the council, it later became clear that the plurality of religions was one of the most significant realities of our time, one that constituted a vigorous challenge to our theology.

With regard to world religions, the response involved welcoming others who were different, foreign, or even irreconcilable. I have no doubt that theology today has to find a way to be hospitable to other religions, to welcome the stranger. I therefore want to give special attention to this approach, and I begin by calling attention to some precursors who practiced this kind of hospitality.

Serge de Beaurecueil (1917–1998)

Father Serge de Laugier de Beaurecueil should certainly be numbered among the pioneers of the church's encounter with Islam.

In the context of the church's relation to Islam, mention must also be made of Blessed Charles de Foucauld (1859–1916). He lived at a time when no explicit interreligious dialogue was imaginable, but by choosing to immerse himself among the Tuaregs, he was a forerunner of and inspiration for those who were able to go further in their encounter with other believers. Today we recognize that his testimony had a huge influence on the attitude of Christians. We should also mention Louis Massignon, his friend, a scholar and specialist in Islamic mysticism, as well as a celebrated defender of the rights of the weakest, and Father Albert Peyriguère. We could go on, but this is not the place to draw up an exhaustive list.

The experience of Serge de Beaurecueil makes us aware of a different kind of pioneer. He was a Dominican priest who was trained in the academic study of the writings of Muslim mystics, especially Khwaja Abdullah Ansari, an Afghan mystic of the eleventh century. His study gradually led him to a profound affinity with that holy man. In 1956, during a visit to the mausoleum of Ansari in Herat, he decided to remain in Afghanistan with those who were followers of this tradition, especially the poorest. His house, located on the periphery of Kabul, was open to all—street children, beggars, the disabled. At night, this "priest of the non-Christians," as he liked to be called, lifted up all these people to God in prayer, so that the reign of God might come to fulfillment.[9]

Seven years later, in 1963, he was invited by a young neighbor to "share bread and salt," that is to say, to receive the rite of hospitality that fully admitted him as a member of the local community. The initiative came from a Muslim neighbor. He in turn invited his friend to share bread and salt in his own home, sealing a true friendship.[10]

He then began a reflection on hospitality and its strictly theological significance. At that time, before the council, attempts were being made to discern what in other religions was already a preparation for the Gospel. In those parts of the world where evangelism in the sense of an explicit presentation of the Christian mystery was not yet possible, there was talk of "pre-evangelization." It was in this sense that the mission of Father de Foucauld was being interpreted. But meditating on the mystery of hospitality in the light of his experience of sharing bread with a Muslim friend, which for him was like a sacrament, Serge de Beaurecueil saw the need to go further: "The essential message of the Lord is in this sharing. . . . If that is done, *it is enough.*" Even when it took place with a Muslim, it called forth the presence of Christ. "In order for the harvest to be made ready, in order for the birds to find shade, *it is necessary and sufficient* that this contact

[9] Serge de Beaurecueil, *Prêtre des non-chrétiens* (Paris: Cerf, 1968).
[10] Serge de Beaurecueil, *Nous avons partagé le pain et le sel* (Paris: Cerf, 1965).

with the earth take place, it is necessary and sufficient that the grain be buried there."[11]

His welcoming of others in Kabul was not just pre-evangelization; it was already the wordless but effective realization of the kingdom. The "theology of fulfillment" that *Nostra ætate* would develop was therefore already passé.

In an article published in 1975 titled "Meditation on My House," he says that in his house in Kabul the "sacred" was originally concentrated in his chapel but then gradually spread to all the rooms where he welcomed his guests. Thanks to hospitality, "the house itself became a temple, a temple for everyone."[12]

Serge de Beaurecueil wrote few books and articles apart from his studies on Ansari. He is much less well-known than Le Saux or Merton. By his example, however, he helped many people understand that the full dimension of hospitality involved welcoming other religions.

We must sadly conclude our presentation of one who was so passionately attached to Afghanistan by noting that in 1983, four years after the Soviet invasion, he was expelled from the country.

Interreligious Dialogue and Hospitality

The intuitions of Serge de Beaurecueil are very helpful in understanding how necessary interreligious encounter is for the whole of theology, especially interreligious encounter as an expression of hospitality. As a way of prolonging his reflections, I want to describe how hospitality contributes to a theology of interreligious encounter.

[11] Ibid., 66 and 73 (emphasis in the original).
[12] In Serge de Beaurecueil, *Je crois en l'étoile du matin* (Paris: Cerf, 2005), 43.

Lately, many authors who speak of interreligious dialogue encourage taking the "risk of hospitality"[13] in order to encounter other believers completely.[14]

Hospitality always involves a risk. The Indo-European root "host" is at the origin of the word "hospitality" but also of the word "hostility." Guests, strangers, might be enemies; at any rate, they are always a risk. To practice hospitality, we must overcome fear and stand up to condemnation. Since hospitality requires breaking down barriers, it has always been considered sacred.

Looking more closely at the characteristics of this way of acting, we see how it can be applied to interreligious encounter.

Hospitality is less explicit than dialogue, but it is more existential, involving our life in a very concrete way. It assumes a minimum of verbal exchange, but in return, it may bring new intensity to dialogue. The two complement each other well.

In fact, the precise meaning of hospitality is that one welcomes a stranger as a stranger, recognizing his or her difference, and thereby eliminating the danger of amalgamation. Guests who are welcomed in such a manner know that they are not at home and must therefore show a certain reserve vis-à-vis their host. This type of meeting is also particularly demanding because it consists in welcoming strangers not *in spite of* everything about them that is irreconcilable but *with* everything about them that cannot be assimilated. In short, it involves encountering the whole person.

---

[13] Martin E. Marty, *When Faiths Collide* (Oxford: Blackwell, 2005), 124.

[14] Catherine Cornille, *The Im-Possibility of Interreligious Dialogue* (New York: Crossroad/Herder & Herder, 2008), 177. We should also mention Richard Kearney, *Anatheism: Returning to God after God* (New York: Columbia University Press, 2011).

It should also be made clear that hospitality in the strict sense is not a right. Guests are not received because they are members of the family or fellow citizens, nor because of their ability to pay, as is the case with a hotel or hospital. They are received for one reason only: *they are in need.* What motivates and even requires hospitality is the poverty of the one who seeks shelter.

If kindness toward the poor is to be truly hospitable, it can never be patronizing. The tradition that has come down to us speaks of the sacred nature of the guest, of a mysterious coincidence between the poor person and God. In welcoming the stranger, it is always the Lord whom we welcome. That conviction is present is the most varied religious traditions. Chapter 53 of the Rule of Saint Benedict summarizes Christian teaching on this subject when it says that "all guests" are to be received as messengers of God and that in those who come, "Christ is adored," for he will say, "I was a stranger and you welcomed me" (Matt 25:35). According to the language of Christian theology, it can be said that hospitality is a "theological" reality in the sense that—like faith, hope, or charity—its object is God.

Hospitality thus appears as a privileged way to meet the follower of another religion. This is all the more true since hospitality is known and respected as sacred in all cultures and religions. One could cite many, often remarkable, texts from ancient Egypt and Babylon, and from Homer, the Upanishads, the Dhammapada, or Ovid, to mention only the most ancient. The hospitality of Abraham, narrated in chapter 18 of Genesis, is an especially well-known text from the biblical tradition. But this is not the place to compile an anthology.[15]

---

[15] I have devoted some pages to outstanding examples of hospitality in *Interreligious Hospitality: The Fulfillment of Dialogue*, trans. Robert Henry (Collegeville, MN: Liturgical Press, 2010), 100–107.

Before exploring the conditions and challenges of interreligious hospitality, we need to stress one last feature of hospitality that makes it so demanding, especially when offered in an interreligious context. In French, the word *hôte* is ambiguous. It can refer either to the one who invites or to the one invited. But this ambiguity is essential. Hospitality has two sides, depending on whether one is giving or receiving it.

Usually one speaks about the hospitality that is offered, and most books on the subject are devoted almost exclusively to this dimension. However, the hospitality that is requested and received is just as important. The two are not only complementary; they are constitutive. If one of the two is missing, hospitality is not only incomplete but also distorted. The proof of this is that we cannot welcome a guest if we ourselves have not experienced the need to be accepted. That is why it is written in the law of Moses, "You shall love the alien as yourself, for you were aliens in the land of Egypt" (Lev 19:34). If we do not remember any experience of being an alien, we will probably not even notice that there are aliens in our midst! In any case, it would be difficult to show them genuine respect. We should therefore always ask ourselves if we have received enough to be able to give without any risk of arrogance—whatever our good intentions. This is especially important for interreligious hospitality.

Moreover, in the opinion of all those who risked offering hospitality, the experience on the side of the one who asks for it is almost always much more significant. Hospitality is certainly a moral duty—one could even say that it is the foundation of all morality—but hospitality received is a greater spiritual experience, since it is unmerited and freely given.

All the pioneers of interreligious dialogue actually began in this way. Le Saux made a decisive step on his path of interreligious encounter the day he left Shantivanam, his Christian monastery, to live in the ashram of Rāmana Maharshi in Tiruvanamalai and with Swami Gñānānanda in Tirukkoyilur.

For each of the pioneers, it would be appropriate to indicate the moment when they began their exodus and asked to join with the believers of other religious traditions, for it was then that their conversion was realized.

Evangelical Hospitality

In accepting the hospitality of others, these pioneers were simply putting the Gospel into practice. Indeed, the Gospel tradition is very clear. However, you have to have had a profound experience of hospitality to grasp all that is implied therein.

When Jesus sent his disciples to proclaim the inbreaking of the kingdom, he ordered them to take no provisions and to depend on alms (see Matt 10 and Luke 9 and 10). If he asked them to take nothing with them, "no gold, or silver, or copper in your belts, no bag for your journey, or two tunics, or sandals, or a staff," this is not, as is commonly said, so that they could practice asceticism by being detached from material goods. Rather, Jesus is asking them to be dependent, forced to ask for help from others, forced to rely on the generosity of their hosts. He orders them to "enter the house with a greeting of peace." Furthermore, they are to stay there "eating and drinking whatever they provide." This way of behaving, which is so carefully described, is not just a way of winning goodwill. Nor is it just a prelude to the proclamation of the kingdom of God. The hospitality thus requested and received is already an announcement of the kingdom, the firstfruits of the Gospel, a manifestation of the "God who is in need of human beings." Hospitality given and received makes it possible for those who welcome the disciples to hear the truth of their proclamation, "The Kingdom of God has come upon you."

Jesus himself lived this way after he left his home in Nazareth. With his disciples, he went from village to village, relying on the kindness of others, but not always sure of finding shelter. As Jesus said, the Son of Man had "nowhere to lay his head" (Luke 9:58), and he proposed that the apostles should put themselves in the same situation when they went out to preach the Good News. In the Acts of the Apostles we can see how his recommendations were followed, and how doing so offered unlimited possibilities for the work of evangelization.

Unfortunately, this way of evangelizing was not followed in the post-apostolic period. As the church grew more and more powerful, politically and materially, it became self-sufficient, closed in on itself, and even aggressive vis-à-vis all others. Eventually, the church became "tribalized," identifying the Christian faith with the vision of its own closed world, Christendom. This lamentable drift away from the Gospel is mainly a consequence of neglecting Christ's counsel to his disciples that they should first seek hospitality. The culmination of this drift toward self-sufficiency was that the church forgot that being hospitable had priority over other demands. Instead of the practice of sacred hospitality, it was often the practice of rejection that was held to be sacred!

The church went so far as to restore archaic prohibitions against believers of other religions. By appealing to the most virulent expression of xenophobia in some parts of the Bible, Christians came to understand and practice the proclamation of the faith to the Gentiles as the first stage of a war of conquest. The only way to save the heathen was to subjugate them. Is it not surprising that during all these centuries of Christendom, the missionaries of the Gospel, who were so eager to proclaim Christ—sometimes at the cost of their own lives—did not believe they had a duty to obey the very specific directions that the Lord had given them as to *how* to announce this Good News? They were so puffed up with the assurance that their point of view was superior to all others that they were unable to hear the explicit requirement placed on them by the Gospel. And yet, even though they announced Jesus Christ in their own way, the power of the Gospel message still took root in the hearts of their hearers "night and day" (Mark 4:27).

Today we have been healed of some of this self-sufficiency, and we can rediscover the relevance of the path of hospitality for every kind of encounter.

Still, this focus on hospitality in interreligious encounter may raise some eyebrows. Are we not manipulating these texts by applying them to a situation that Christ did not have in mind? If he sent his disciples on mission, it was to preach the Good News, not to sympathize with the believers of other religions! Is the way of hospitality, then, a legitimate one, or is it, in fact, an evasion of the injunction to be missionaries that eventually leads to a veritable "decommissioning"?

It is not possible to answer this question in general terms, because there are as many answers as there are situations. In some cases, Christians are called to give explicit and unequivocal testimony. In other cases—which today are more and more frequent—explicit proclamation is not possible. We therefore have to adapt the ways of witnessing to the Gospel. We must remember that in the church gifts vary according to the person and the circumstances. Not everyone is capable of all that goes into the proclamation of the Gospel, but all are involved in this mission in one way or another.

It is clear that witnesses like Le Saux did not engage in dialogue out of curiosity, or out of spite, or because they needed a change! Their "exodus" and their life choices were dictated by motivations that were religious, and specifically evangelical. This choice, however, excluded any desire to convince, change, and convert their interlocutors. They were not ashamed of the Gospel (see Rom 1:16), but they sincerely believed that the best way to preach it was by the radiance of their joy. They proclaimed the Gospel like the woman of the parable who had found her silver coin. She called together

her friends and neighbors to share her joy (Luke 15:8-10). In their own way and in their own surroundings they gave witness to Christ. Even though individuals such as Enomiya Lassalle or Serge de Beaurecueil did not have the charism of preaching the Word explicitly, they have always been recognized as witnesses to Christ and his church. As de Beaurecueil wrote, "The only way any word will be accepted is *if it is a response*."[16] In a multireligious context the only statement that can be heard is the one that responds to a question prompted by the witness given by Christians, especially their hospitality.

That said, we must remember that the question of the proper relationship between dialogue and mission remains delicate. It was taken up extensively in a document jointly prepared by the Pontifical Council for Interreligious Dialogue and the Congregation for the Evangelization of Peoples, titled "Dialogue and Proclamation."[17]

This brief treatment of evangelical hospitality should make it clear that hospitality is an ideal *locus* for the development of a theology of interreligious encounter. It is not the only *locus*, but it has the advantage of always combining theory and practice. Let us then take a closer look at the major revisions that are required in a theology of interreligious dialogue if it is to be more in line with the Gospel.

New Paths for Theology

I would like to point out some of the theological approaches that have already been shaped by the experiences and reflections of the past years. As we embark on the path of theolog-

[16] Serge de Beaurecueil, *Nous avons partagé le pain et le sel* (Paris: Cerf, 1965), 77; emphasis in the original.

[17] Accessible on the website of the Holy See: http://www.vatican.va/roman_curia/pontifical_councils/interelg/documents/rc_pc_interelg_doc_19051991_dialogue-and-proclamatio_en.html.

ical conversion, there are three all-important steps to be taken: changing the way we see things; consenting to a certain impoverishment; and, finally, sharing unconditionally.

Changing the Way We See Things

Theology today is invited to change the way it regards those outside the church. In some cases what will be required is even a complete change of perspective. Theology can no longer be self-referential; it can no longer judge everything from the center. The view from outside is indispensable.

To bring about this change, it is first of all necessary to make an important distinction. *Agape*, evangelical love, is shown in two ways, depending on the circumstances. It is love of the brother and sister, *philadelphia*, but it is also love of the stranger, *philoxenia*, the opposite of xenophobia. Let it be noted that *philoxenia* is the Greek word for hospitality!

These two expressions of the same love are quite different. The first tends to unanimity; the other respects diversity. The first leads to tacit agreement and therefore the silence of consent; the second never relinquishes speech. The approaches are different, but love for one who is far away demands no less than love for the neighbor. The difference between these two forms of *agape* is not of degree but of kind.

The Christian tradition has always preferred the love of neighbor, which tends toward unanimity and obedience. Led by a rather naively egocentric view of reality, it looked on *philoxenia*, love for one who is more distant, as an extension of *philadelphia* and then, in some way, a substitute for it. Instead of respecting the stranger as stranger, as one who is different by definition, Christians thought they honored strangers by offering to assimilate and integrate them into their own universe. Christians tried to make those who were far off into neighbors, thinking that was the only way they could be recognized and saved. Meanwhile, this concern, if

not obsession, led to the imposition of unanimity and ortho-
doxy. Instead of rejoicing in diversity, Christians regarded
whatever was different as inadequate. In the end, difference
became a justification for exclusion. In any case, there was
no question of receiving anything at all from others.

Today, however, we really do want to receive the other
without seeking to make the other "one of us." As Pope Francis said to the diplomatic corps shortly after his election, "It
is not possible to establish true links with God, while ignoring
other people."[18] *Philoxenia* has to be recuperated and restored
to its place at the center of Christian life and theology.

Certainly, there are ways believers from another tradition
can be close to us, especially when we discover a real meeting
of hearts and minds about the values we hold most precious.
But if we are to respect them fully, we must also take into
account the vast differences between our respective traditions, even the inconsistencies that make us strangers to one
another.

The conversion necessary for a profound encounter with
believers of other religions, however, goes even further. It
requires an exodus, such as we saw in the lives of the great
witnesses of interreligious encounter. It is not enough to go
to the very frontiers of our world; sometimes we have to be
willing to leave it behind.

Here again the Gospel opens up new perspectives. In the
parable of the Good Samaritan, Jesus proposes a radical reversal. In concluding this story, he turns around the question
posed by the doctor of the Law. It is the wounded man who
must be foremost in our attention, not our own moral per-
fection. Instead of asking "What will happen to me if I stop

---

[18] Audience with the Diplomatic Corps Accredited to the Holy See,
March 22, 2013. On the website of the Holy See: http://w2.vatican.va
/content/francesco/en/speeches/2013/march/documents/papa
-francesco_20130322_corpo-diplomatico.html.

to take care of the injured man?" his question must be, "What would happen to him if I didn't stop?"

To encounter others, we have to turn away from our own interests and concerns and put ourselves in their shoes. That can only happen if we remember that we too are, in part, strangers, waiting for a home. Indeed, to "put ourselves in somebody else's shoes" is not role playing. It does not mean taking on an assumed identity but becoming aware of what we really are, at least in certain respects.

Commenting on the hospitality the Patriarch Abraham offered three visitors (see Gen 18), St. Augustine says that when you receive a guest, you receive a companion for the journey, because on earth we are all travelers. If Abraham is rightly regarded as the model of hospitality, is it not because he was able to say to the people of Hebron, "I am a stranger and an alien residing among you" (Gen 23:4)? Since that time, it is true, we have settled in. The Christian tradition established itself in well-defined regions of the Greco-Roman world and in some neighboring regions, and it developed wonderfully. We can say that our Christian spiritual tradition has become a large house, established on solid foundations, and we can be happy about that. But our happiness will only be complete if our house becomes a place that is truly welcoming.

By welcoming others, we discover that the church is not necessarily the center of everything. When Pope Paul VI established secretariats for dialogue in 1964, the model for them was that of concentric circles: the first was for non-Catholics, the second for non-Christians, and the third for unbelievers. It was only in 1988, after twenty-five years of experience, that these organizations received new names, one of them being the Pontifical Council for Interreligious Dialogue. In this area too there has been a Copernican revolution.

Finally, we should note that this new way of referring to them is not only friendly but also caring and confident. In the same way, theology will not be fully transformed until it offers unconditional welcome. Personal conviction is necessary, but it should not cause us to hesitate in showing hospitality. If we hold back, more or less consciously and intentionally, communication is impeded and access to a deeper level is roped off. On the other hand, when theologians recognize that all religions have an important word to say about God and a life oriented toward the Absolute, theology becomes more humble, and therefore more real and credible.

Accepting Poverty

The discovery of other spiritual traditions is first of all an opportunity for enrichment, especially when in the course of this encounter we discover very beautiful texts, images, methods, or moving rituals. When we allow ourselves to be deeply moved by the testimony of sages and saints we have met, we also come to the realization that our own spiritual treasures are being challenged when they are compared to these other riches. Furthermore, if we have the good fortune of a friendly encounter with someone who practices another spiritual tradition with great fervor, much of our certainty about the absolute value of our Christian path is undermined.

Many of the clarifications that churches have felt obliged to add over the centuries to defend and explain the Christian tradition now appear irrelevant or unnecessary. In the course of our respectful encounters with followers of other traditions we begin to see how the churches' *a priori* assessment of these traditions and the exclusive claims they make for themselves are little more than a manifestation of ignorance, not only of the true nature of other religions, but even more, of the beyond-thought-and-word reality of any religion. It simply is not possible to make comparisons between the ways spiritual realities are expressed by different traditions, since one cannot be completely immersed in both. It is even less acceptable to establish a hierarchy of values among the various spiritual traditions. The only thing one can legitimately compare is the conduct of the followers of these traditions.

Finally, as we saw with the monks who were pioneers of dialogue, their experience was one of letting things settle and of impoverishment. Their poverty, however, was not destitution and spiritual misery! In dialogue, the essentials of the faith appear more clearly, and the desire for a spiritual quest inspired by the Gospel is greatly intensified. Those who live this kind of poverty of spirit are also blessed!

This discovery, which is furthered by interreligious encounter, also supports the development of the spiritual life. To the extent that we deepen our spiritual experience, we discover that faith is, above all, a quest. This awareness makes possible a deeper encounter. When, in either a silent or a verbal exchange, we can share the experience of an ever-unsatisfied thirst for God or Truth, our communion with one another can be very intense.

To illustrate what is involved in the encounter between religions, the image of people climbing a mountain is frequently evoked. The climbers take different paths, but eventually they all come together at the top. I beg to differ. The reality is not that simple. If you want to keep the image of a mountain, I would propose that it be a volcano. The climbers take different paths, but when they reach the top, they discover a cauldron, a sea of fire that is absolutely impassable. What attracts everyone also keeps them apart. What brings us together is what is beyond us.

Here too, spiritual experience orients and modifies theological research. Theology is a word about God, no doubt. Therefore, it cannot be silent. However, the more immersed it is in the experience of the Unutterable, and the more this experience is lived in communion with others, its word about God can be even stronger, a word that calls to conversion.

Sharing Unconditionally

Hospitality is essentially reciprocal. Among the instructions that Christ gives his disciples when he sends them out to announce the kingdom, he tells them to eat and drink what their hosts serve them and to remain in their house as long as necessary. In exchange for the Gospel they announce, those who are sent receive all these signs of hospitality. But should we limit these signs to material food and a roof over one's head? In an interreligious context, should not those who speak to people of other faiths, doing so discreetly, also let it be known that they, in turn, are willing to be nourished by the spiritual food that sustains their hosts? If we are really to meet them, we need to take to heart and appreciate their reasons for living: their scriptures, their sacred dwellings, and their spiritual traditions. In fact, we see that the pioneers of dialogue drank deeply from the Upanishads, the Dhammapada, or the Qur'an. This experience even allowed them to renew their appreciation for the Bible. St. Paul remarks that Christian love "rejoices in the truth" (1 Cor 13:6). No matter where it comes from, truth causes admiration and joy. Massignon was able to write,

> Truth is a pure and serene spiritual relationship between two partners who understand one another (Plato), as when a stranger becomes a host. . . . It is only insofar as one offers hospitality to others (instead of colonizing them), only insofar as we share the same work and the same bread, that we become aware of the truth that unites us. The only way to discover truth is by practicing hospitality.[19]

In the gospels we see that Jesus began by taking into account the concerns of those he met. He constantly asked, "What do you think?" (Matt 18:12; 21:28); "Have you under-

---

[19] Louis Massignon, *Opera Minora* (Paris: Presses Universitaires de France, 1969), t. III, p. 586.

stood all this?" (Matt 13:51); "Why do you not judge for your-
selves what is right?" (Luke 12:57). His words were also
"hospitable words," even when they were harsh and challenging, because they were preceded by accepting the questions of those with whom he was speaking. His word was all
the more relevant since it was given with full knowledge of
what was being asked.

The practice of interreligious dialogue can only encourage
the development of what might be called a "hospitable theology." This is not to say that our theology should welcome
everything and anything, but it should be markedly different
from one that is primarily concerned about what it needs to
exclude. For centuries doctrine was "defined" by exclusion,
specifying the boundaries beyond which the faith was in
danger and the faithful ultimately doomed to condemnation.
By relating to the real world objectively and respectfully, as
Pope John XXIII wanted the Second Vatican Council to do,
this way of presenting the faith was finally abandoned and
we discarded the terrible formula *anathema sit* that used to
conclude any doctrinal decree.

Now we can fully receive our dialogue partners and welcome them as guests and thus messengers of God. As paradoxical as it may seem, someone who practices another
religion can sometimes help us to live our own tradition better. History will say that a hospitable theology brings about
a better understanding of the Mystery.

There is an image that beautifully summarizes all of these
reflections on a theology of hospitality. It is the icon of the
hospitality of Abraham, the most famous of which is the Trinity of Saint Sergius written by Andre Rublev. It is significant
that in the East this episode from the life of Abraham was
chosen to represent the Trinity. Unlike Western iconography
of the Trinity, which mainly expresses majesty and power,
the icon of divine *philoxenia* illustrates rather the movement
and the gift of hospitality, *perichoreisis*, that unites the three

Persons. Is it not remarkable that Eastern theology has chosen the image of mutual hospitality to represent the love burning at the very heart of the Trinity?

Whatever we do to become more welcoming, let us not lose sight of this truth. All of our expressions of hospitality ultimately have their source in the living God.

3

Interreligious Prayer

Interreligious prayer is at the heart of the encounter between believers of different religions. It is not only at the heart of such an encounter; it is the goal. *Communicatio in sacris*—that is to say, participation in the sacred functions of another denomination or religion—was once considered a sacrilege. A few decades ago Catholics were even forbidden to pray the Our Father with Protestants! In response to this ban, Raimon Panikkar used to insist that there is no real communication unless it be *in sacris*. It is at this level that communication becomes communion.

The Testimony of Tibhirine

Beginning in the nineteenth century, French Trappists founded several monasteries in the colonies: in Syria, the Congo, and a little later at Tibhirine in Algeria. In 1963 the Abbot General decided to close the monastery in Algeria because the community was entirely French and it seemed to be little more than a remnant of a bygone era. However, most of the brothers decided to stay with Brother Luke, a physician who tirelessly served the local community. The spirit of the monastery changed, especially with the arrival of Father Christian de Chergé in 1971. The personality of the man who would soon become the prior of the community was certainly decisive, but it is important to recall that the option for full solidarity with the population of the village was made by the whole community.[1] The monks were not involved in explicit dialogue on matters of faith with their neighbors, but they were very much a part of the religious life of the village. They even offered a place within the monastic grounds for a mosque.

The strength of this monastery was its prayer, and prayer is what made for such a strong bond with the surrounding population. The monks did not just pray for their Muslim neighbors; they wanted to pray with them. De Chergé recounts that the initiative for these more explicit moments of common prayer came from the Sufi Muslims who had created a prayer group called *Ribāt-es-Salām* (the bond of peace). According to Bruno Chenu, these Muslims said to the monks,

> We do not want to engage with you in a doctrinal discussions. In the area of dogma or theology, human beings create many barriers. But we feel called to unity. We want to let God create something new among us. This can only be done in prayer. That is why we want to meet with you in prayer.[2]

Christian de Chergé had already had an experience of praying with Muslims. He recalled an encounter he had with a Muslim guest in 1975. They had both remained in the monastery chapel one evening after the office of Compline.

---

[1] John Kiser, *The Monks of Tibhirine: Faith, Love, and Terror in Algeria* (New York: Macmillan, 2003).

[2] Bruno Chenu, ed., *Sept vies pour Dieu et l'Algérie* (Paris: Bayard, 1996), 35.

Ours was a single prayer in two voices. Arabic and French intermingle, are mysteriously joined together, melt and merge, complement and combine with one another. Lord, One and Almighty, You who see us, You who unite everything under your eyes, Lord of tenderness and mercy, God, our God, our only God. Teach us to pray together, You who alone are the Master of prayer, You who are the first to draw to Yourself those who turn to You.[3]

The witness of Tibhirine is very precious. The monks wanted nothing more than to be "prayerful among those who pray" and thus had forged unbreakable ties with those living around them. This dialogue in and through prayer was brutally ended by the assassination of seven of the monks, but their testimony was not buried with them; it became even stronger. Other believers all over the world sensed that they were called to continue along this path. They realized that, beyond the violence that is today so prevalent, prayer is the strongest bond because it joins us to God. Prayer is the shortest distance between human beings, because God is the one who is closest to us. In our broken and divided world prayer really is "the bond of peace." Today there continue to be small Cistercian communities, for example in Morocco, that continue on in this spirit.

The Day of Prayer for Peace in Assisi, October 27, 1986

Nostra ætate opened the horizons of the church by inviting it to be in dialogue with other religions. In Assisi, barely twenty years later, the holy Pope John Paul II went a step further by offering hospitality to other religions. However, taking into consideration those Christians who were not ready for the full implications of such a gesture, he limited its scope.

[3] Christian de Chergé, *L'invincible espérance* (Paris: Bayard, 1997), 34–35.

Nonetheless, it was undoubtedly a historic event. This was the first time in human history that religions welcomed one another *as religions*—not just as moral, cultural, or societal agencies working for peace in the world, but as praying communities, that is to say, people who strive to enter into communion with the Absolute in order to call down the peace that comes from above. The implication of this mutual recognition is that all religions are "compatible" at a deep level. Communication, even communion, with one another is possible.

The invitation came from the Catholic pope—it was necessary that someone do the inviting—but his guests were free to accept it and to participate in accord with their own convictions.

By proposing to invite representatives of all religions to come together to pray for peace, the pope had taken a prophetic initiative whose implications he was well aware of. In order not to upset the faithful, he agreed to a nuanced description of the day. It would be a time when all would "come together to pray," rather than "come to pray together"! In fact, all those who gathered at the foot of the Basilica of St. Francis joined together in one prayer. I was there, and I can attest that we prayed together. If we reduce prayer to its formulas, it is clear that prayers are different. But at Assisi everyone participated together in all the prayers. Each one entered into the prayer that was led by a particular religious group and made it part of his or her own prayer. The gathering was a wonderful expression of hospitality in prayer. That is why this day is so important in the history of the encounter of religions.

For the benefit of those not easily swayed by his convictions, his closest collaborators in particular, the pope then clarified his thinking in his Christmas address to the Roman Curia:

Every authentic prayer is called forth by the Holy Spirit, who "helps us in our weakness; for we do not know how to

pray as we ought" and who prays in us "with sighs too deep
for words. And God, who searches the heart, knows what
is the mind of the Spirit" (Rom 8:26-27). Indeed, all authentic
prayer is prompted by the Holy Spirit who is mysteriously
present in every human heart.[4]

There were other occasions when the pope again expressed
this conviction, reminding his hearers that the initiative of
Assisi was in line with the teaching of the Second Vatican
Council. It must be admitted, however, that the authors of
Nostra ætate and the bishops who voted for it probably never
imagined a development of this kind. What took place at
Assisi was, in fact, the implementation of a new theological
approach that had been inaugurated by the council and then
had evolved considerably.

All Christians were not represented in Assisi in 1986. The
leaders of certain Protestant denominations had refused to
participate. For Catholics and the great majority of Christians,
however, this kind of interreligious prayer was seen to be
possible and legitimate. The objections raised by certain theologians are not convincing. It is significant, however, that at
other interreligious meetings organized by the Vatican, participants from other religions have been given a warm welcome and beautiful words have been spoken, but there has
been no common prayer. Perhaps it was felt necessary to
observe a moratorium in such a delicate area.

The Pontifical Council for Interreligious Dialogue and the
Office on Interreligious Relations of the World Council of
Churches organized a joint theological consultation on this
issue. I was able to attend and shared the experience of

---

[4] Speech to the Roman Curia, December 1986. The Italian text is given
on the Vatican website: http://w2.vatican.va/content/john-paul-ii
/it/speeches/1986/december/documents/hf_jp-ii_spe_19861222
_curia-romana.html.

monks. The conclusions of the two meetings, held in Bangalore (India) and Bose (Italy), were published in 1998.[5]

This document noted that prayer is indeed a universal phe-
nomenon but that it is equally an intimate activity, carried
out in the heart of each believer. Our understanding of the
universal dimension of prayer does not mean we can impose
it on believers for whom prayer has an exclusive quality. We
need only remember those Christians who preferred to die
rather than participate in pagan worship by offering incense
before the statues of the deified emperors. Today the situation
has changed and the interpretation of peoples' actions is not
always so clear cut. For example, in some settings we can feel
free to join Buddhists in the recitation of a Buddhist sutra
because they know that this does not imply any disavowal
of our Christian faith. But in most cases we cannot assume
that we know what the reactions of believers of other religions will be.

The great respect that is required of us in the area of prayer
is expressed by great restraint. We cannot presume that we
are welcome at the worship of another religious tradition; we
need to be explicitly invited. Nor is it fitting to "salvage"
beautiful prayers from another tradition by simply inserting
the name of God in the original text. Nor is it advisable to
incorporate prayers from another religion in the *regular* liturgical prayer of a community, as some have tried to do. On
occasion, however, it is quite appropriate to include sacred
texts from other traditions in order to give our daily prayer
a note of universality.

As we see, this area is delicate and the possible pitfalls are
many. Nonetheless, while taking into account all these warnings, interreligious prayer is desirable. Sometimes it is even
necessary, as, for instance, when a tragic event strikes a region

[5] "Interreligious Prayer: A Joint Study," *Pro Dialogo* 98, no. 2 (1998).

whose population is multireligious. It would be regrettable not to include all the people affected, allowing them to bring this event before the Absolute in order to make some sense of it. Shared prayer also has a place in smaller groups that meet regularly for dialogue.

Prayer in such a setting can be a juxtaposition of prayers from different religious traditions in which all participate to the extent possible, as was the case at Assisi. The choice of a unified prayer, that is to say, one that is already interreligious in its formulation, is riskier. In seeking to express the highest common denominator between very different traditions, the prayer usually ends up expressing vague generalities that no one really owns. In multireligious settings there will often be a place for common gestures that can be apt expressions of common prayer. Often the best solution is silent prayer set off by some brief evocations of prayers from different traditions.

In any event, it is essential that those who have decided to pray together work together to prepare for the occasion, and that they do so carefully, because what they are doing is very new and therefore unfamiliar.

The venue is also significant. Rather than choosing a neutral setting, it is better to choose the place of worship of a particular community. In this case, the laws of hospitality indicate that the meeting places be varied, so that each community has a chance to be both host and guest.

Even if, for practical reasons, interreligious prayer is exceptional, the mere fact that it is possible is a valuable contribution to the practice of prayer. The representative of the Zoroastrian religion at the Assisi meeting told me as we were returning to Rome the next day, "My prayer will no longer be like it was before. I will no longer be able to pray without remembering that so many others are praying like me."

The new dimension of faith is most remarkably manifested when the heart is expanded by interreligious prayer.

Trans-religious Meditation

So far I have only spoken about sharing prayers that are recited, sung, or involve bodily movement. There is also the possibility of interfaith communion in the practice of prayer that is completely silent. This form of prayer or meditation often makes for an encounter that is more engaging, but not without risk. Nontheless, it is practiced by many Christians.

To be sure, there are some who are content to borrow for their own spiritual benefit methods developed in Hindu and Buddhist circles and to remain untouched by the original religious context in which these methods were developed. Such borrowing is legitimate, since these methods are part of the cultural heritage of humanity and are therefore available to all. However, simply to avail oneself of treasures that have been amassed by generations of spiritual practitioners is an approach that is somewhat consumerist. Moreover, because they intentionally avoid any contact with the spiritual milieu in which these methods were developed, these Christians lose a valuable opportunity for a fruitful encounter.

Such an encounter, however, requires that one pay the price, as can be seen in the lives of some pioneers of the dialogue of spiritual experience, one of whom we turn to now.

Enomiya Lassalle (1898–1990)

Father Hugo Lassalle was born into a very Catholic family, whose ancestry, however, was Huguenot. He shared the fate of all his compatriots in the German Empire. In 1916 he was drafted and sent to the Western Front, where he was wounded. Unable to continue in the military, he entered the Jesuit novitiate shortly after he was discharged.

In 1929, at his express request, he was sent to Japan as a missionary. There he devoted himself to social ministry in favor of the most marginalized members of society. In his desire to become ever more Japanese with the Japanese, he decided to learn about their religion. In 1943, he participated for the first time in a *sesshin* (meditation retreat) in a Zen monastery.

On August 6, 1945, he was in Hiroshima, actually only 1,500 meters away from ground zero, when the atomic bomb fell. The house he was in protected him from radiation, but he was wounded by falling debris. Nonetheless, he hastened to help his compatriots in any way he could. Three years later, he became a Japanese citizen and took the name Enomiya Makibi.

It was only after 1950 that he resumed his study of Zen Buddhism, becoming a disciple of Daiun Sogaku Harada in 1956. He deliberately sought spiritual hospitality in Zen Buddhism. As he wrote in his diary, "My goal now is to get into the Zen Buddhist world—literally inside it, like going inside a house in order to participate in the life of the house."[6] With rigor and tenacity, he then launched into a historical and practical study of Zen and eventually was officially recognized as a member of one of the branches of Soto Zen Buddhism.

He then decided to pass on his discoveries to others, inviting them to a deeper intellectual and experiential knowledge of Zen Buddhism. As might be expected, his first book,[7] published in 1960, was immediately taken off the market by order of his superiors. It was only after the Second Vatican Council that he could speak freely. In 1967, for the first time, he organized a Zen *sesshin* in a German Benedictine abbey. Thereafter, he devoted his energy to introducing Christians to contemplative prayer according to the methods of Zen.

---

[6] Ursula Baatz, *Hugo M. Enomiya-Lassalle: ein Leben zwischen den Welten* (Zürich and Düsseldorf: Benzinger Verlag, 1998), 263.

[7] *Zen, Weg zur Erleuchtung*, English translation: *Zen—Way to Enlightenment* (London: Burns and Oates, 1967).

During the last years of his long life, most of his activity consisted of directing *sesshins* throughout Europe. In one of his last books, published in 1980, he clearly stated his agenda:

> I direct my attention to those who have kept their Christian faith and who want to find a way of meditation that is, as far as possible, adapted to their being Christian and to their present human condition, with their inhibitions, troubles and concerns.[8]

Thus, he was essentially speaking to and had a great impact on Christian spirituality. More than anyone else, he helped liberate consciences that were uneasy about this type of dialogue. But he did not really delve deeply into the relationship between the Buddhist and Christian traditions. When he died in 1990, he left many unanswered questions.

The Dialogue of Silence

It is at the level of contemplative prayer that the problems raised by interreligious dialogue appear most clearly, but at the same time, it is also in this area that prospects are especially bright for the future of spiritual dialogue. I am con-

---

[8] H. M. Enomiya-Lassalle, *La méditation comme voie vers l'expérience de Dieu* (Paris: Cerf, 1982), 10. Translation of *Meditation als Weg zur Gottenfahrung*. In the English translation of this work, his intention is stated somewhat differently: "The more I studied Zen, the more clearly I realized its deep influence on Japanese thought. Not content with mere theory, I also practised Zen, taking part in Zen meditations. It was then that I came to realize that Zen was a great help to my own spiritual life. My conviction grew that, practised in the right way, Zen could be useful to anyone regardless of his religious conviction and denomination. The experiences and impression which follow are offered for publication because I think that this method should be made accessible to others" (*Zen—Way to Enlightenment*, 9).

vinced that the experience of meditation according to an Eastern method and in its religious setting is essential to intrareligious dialogue. I therefore believe it is necessary to address this issue more explicitly.

We should not minimize the risks of interreligious encounter at this most intimate level of the spiritual life. In the 1950s, an undertaking such as that attempted by Father Lassalle was deemed impossible. Speaking of Christians who practiced Zen, Hans Urs von Balthasar even described Zen meditation as an outrageous deviation and a veritable treason. "This defection can only be described as a treasonable betrayal of the crucified love of God, and—since we are speaking of the incarnation of God's love—as adultery."[9] This great theologian was not alone. Many others felt the same way. Finally, in 1989, the Congregation for the Doctrine of the Faith felt obliged to intervene by issuing a "Letter to the Bishops of the Catholic Church on some Aspects of Christian Meditation."[10]

All of these often virulent reactions remind us of the seriousness of the issue. Unfortunately, made as they are by outsiders, they show great ignorance of the matter. It is impossible to describe the involvement of Christians who engage in these forms of meditation without adopting an attitude of dialogue, that is to say, without endeavoring to know those who are involved in this way of dialogue and without showing consideration for those who have attempted such an encounter. Here too, without some prior experience of dialogue, theoretical analyses and warnings are not helpful.

[9] Hans Urs von Balthasar, "Une méditation? . . . plutôt une trahison," in *Des bords du Gange aux rives du Jourdain* (Paris and Fribourg: Éditions Saint-Paul, 1983), 154–63.

[10] October 15, 1989. On the website of the Holy See at http://www.vatican.va/roman_curia/congregations/cfaith/documents/rc_con_cfaith_doc_19891015_meditazione-cristiana_en.html.

Father Lassalle made every effort to demonstrate the compatibility of Zen with the Christian mystical tradition. Today, twenty-five years later, the focus is rather on the fruits of a spiritual encounter with a tradition that is radically different from or even incompatible with ours. We have to keep in mind that Zen is rooted in a Buddhist worldview; it is, in fact, one of the purest expressions of Buddhism. We can obviously make use of some of its features, especially its methods of meditation. The practice of *vipassanā*, "insight meditation," has given excellent results in several areas. I am here speaking only of Zen as applied to the whole of one's life and as can be experienced in Zen monasteries. This Zen is not neutral and cannot be replicated with impunity in another spiritual context. That's why one cannot be a "Zen Christian." There can only be Zen practiced by Christians.

In fact, these Christians are now quite numerous. As improbable as it may seem for Christians to practice Zen meditation, it has also proved to be extremely fruitful. It seems to me that it is precisely the shock of coming into contact with a foreign practice that challenges Christians to come forward with what is best in their tradition.

"Meditation without object" is indeed a fundamental challenge to Christian spirituality. One might even call it a provocation, and Thomas Merton was already troubled by it. Paradoxically, it is by drawing spiritual energy from their own faith that Christians can enter on this spiritual path that is in some way at the root of every spiritual quest. It requires a radical purification of the senses and the mind, but it also releases new creativity for living the faith today. Without doubt, important discoveries are still to be made on this path of encounter.

To conclude, we recognize that encountering other religions in prayer is the most fundamental form of dialogue. Obviously, it cannot remain isolated from other forms of encounter and dialogue. It draws them further along.

It is at this stage of dialogue that we can recall the famous adage *lex orandi, lex credendi*,[11] which can be translated as "the way we pray determines the way we believe." Such an adage should not, of course, be absolutized. In the history of theology it has always meant that traditional liturgical formulations are decisive when it comes to determining what constitutes our common faith. In calling up this adage today, theologians also recognize that there is a special relationship between prayer and faith, at least when faith is seen as a journey. But when applied to interreligious prayer, this statement obviously raises serious questions. If some want to "pray with others who pray," to what degree are they involved in the faith journey of those other prayerful people? Can those whose prayer was expanded by spiritual communion with other prayerful people really say that their faith was also expanded? And what is this "faith" that grows through contact with other traditions?

Once again, we are face-to-face with the question of this mysterious "growth" of faith through contact with the other. To continue our reflection, we must therefore devote further study to the concrete way of living this interreligious encounter in depth. We must specify the conditions that are needed if Christian faith is to be strengthened rather than deformed.

---

[11] Prosper of Aquitaine, *Indiculus de gratia Dei*. PL 51:209F. The exact formulation is *Legem credendi lex statuat supplicandi*.

4

A New Conversion to the Gospel

The days of pioneers in foreign lands are past. We can all hear the call to dialogue here and now, in our daily lives. People from foreign lands are our neighbors, and the whole world is now within reach. This actuality fundamentally changes our way of being Christian. Indeed, I believe that it is not just a matter of developing greater respect for and interest in spiritual traditions that exist in other parts of the world. Rather, we need to hear the invitation of St. Paul to the Romans in a new way: "Welcome one another, therefore, just as Christ has welcomed you, for the glory of God" (Rom 15:7). The "others" are no longer only our brothers and sisters and our neighbors but all of our contemporaries who are now so near to us. To do that demands a new conversion, and we need to clarify the practical requirements of such a conversion.

We have seen how the pioneers of dialogue were actually able to experience the changes that occurred in their time as a conversion to the Gospel. Following in their footsteps, we are called to a like conversion by refusing to align ourselves with the current mentality that sees only two possibilities:

the clash of civilizations or miscegenation, or, to put it in other words, exclusion or assimilation. For those who want to become engaged in interreligious dialogue, this false dilemma would suggest that the only two possibilities are conversion to another religion or exploitation of another religion. Sometimes even I find myself thinking, "Without an exclusive adherence to Buddhism, we Christians are incapable of grasping the heart of Buddhism." If that is the case, then the only thing we can do is borrow for our benefit some marginal elements of this tradition—which, morally speaking, is neither very honorable nor spiritually fruitful. We have to refuse this dilemma, because we know that there is a third way. We can testify to the fruitfulness of hospitality at all levels, including that of interreligious dialogue. All the pioneers of interfaith dialogue have enabled us to see that in this spirit, a heart-to-heart encounter is possible, one that fully respects otherness.

We now need to explain how Christians might experience this inner transformation in such a way that their identity is further conformed to the Gospel and not distorted by a pick-and-choose mentality.

To illustrate the process of a radical conversion accomplished "at home," we call on a final witness to shed light on this approach. He did not set out on an "exodus" in the way the pioneers did. Rather, his interfaith encounter took place in his own country, in the depths of his person.

Vincent Shigeto Oshida (1922–2003)

The time has come to listen to the testimony of Asians and Africans, for the Christians of these continents who were and are committed to an interreligious spiritual quest have become witnesses who must be heard. We should also mention here Fathers Aloysius Pieris, SJ, Augustine Ichiro Okumura,

OCD, John Kakishi Kadowaki, SJ, George Anawati, OP, Michael Amaladoss, SJ, and many others, religious and lay. But I limit myself here to one of the clearest witnesses.

"I am a Buddhist who has encountered Christ." That is how Father Oshida referred to himself. He was born into a Buddhist family of the Soto Zen school, and he was barely five when his father taught him sitting meditation (*zazen*). However, he was disappointed by this tradition's lack of discernment in the face of political and military developments in Japan. During his studies he discovered Christianity, and finally, in 1943, he asked to be baptized. After earning a degree in philosophy, he entered the Dominican Order in 1951.

An unforeseen and rather dramatic event would change the course of his life. As he and his companions were swimming in the sea, a wave carried them into the deep. Rescuers brought them all back to shore, but he was the only one who had not drowned.

As he looked for meaning in this close encounter with death, he recognized that in the depth of his being, he had always remained a Buddhist! During the long months of convalescence in a sanatorium, he realized that his conversion to Christianity could in no way demand that he reject his tradition. He did not want to live uprooted, like many of the Japanese Catholics he knew. Instead, he needed to assume the whole of his ancestral tradition, for the glory of God. He later explained:

> I never intended to make Zen a part of my life. That would have been an impossible endeavor. Quite simply, I was born into a family whose father was a Zen Buddhist, and something of that Zen Buddhism was virtually a part of my body and soul since birth. If I can put it this way, Christ made Zen a part of his own life without letting me know. Speaking in a personal way, my Zen master was my illness. There was a time in my long illness when I faced death with deep in-

security. It was then that I saw how much pride I took in my apostolate, which I had thought was an act of pure devotion. Since then I have learned to flee that smell of ego whenever I catch a sniff of it. That was the beginning of Zen in my life.[1]

Father Oshida lived the Gospel in close communion with the suffering and the hopes of his companions in the sanatorium and the poor in the countryside. His fragile health since his near drowning brought him close to all those who were poor and marginalized. With them, most of whom were Buddhist or Shinto, there was no question of interreligious dialogue; there could only be, as he said, "deep communion."

With these friends, he gradually built a community in the "village up the hill," Takamori Soan, a hamlet made of repossessed huts. Their life, punctuated by field work and prayer, was extremely poor, but the place was a haven of peace and hospitality. Those who were welcomed as guests remember the long conversations around the Bible and especially the Eucharist celebrated in one of the small houses. Father Oshida had found a way of celebrating that was altogether Christian and, at the same time, very Japanese; it was as formal as Noh theater and as warm as an agape meal, surprisingly simple, but always based on great interiority. Without resorting to any theory of inculturation, he was, almost unconsciously, 100 percent Christian and 100 percent Japanese and Zen.

Meditation according to the Zen tradition also held an important place at Takamori. The community gathered each day in an improvised zendo to meditate, but, as Father Oshida made clear,

> For me, when I use the word "Zen," one should not interpret it exclusively in the sense of *zazen* or of the Buddhist school

[1] *Enseignements de Vincent Oshida* (Bruxelles: Les Voies de l'Orient, 2009), 22.

of that name, but in its original meaning of *dhyāna* or contemplation. It is in the light of the revelation of Jesus Christ
that I explore Reality with Zen.[2]

He usually led visitors to the spring at Takamori that waters
the fields and all the neighboring villages. It is a sacred spring,
surmounted by a small Shinto shrine. For Father Oshida, it
recapitulated all that is precious and inviolable about nature.
The spring had been in jeopardy because of real estate spec-
ulators who wanted to make it part of an amusement park
and exploit it to sell mineral water. Together with the villag-
ers, he opposed them and even went to court to defend and
protect the spring and the environment. Militancy at the service of respect for creation and for a just life was central in
the life of Father Oshida.

Despite his fragile health, he lived long and had a great
influence on all those who advocate an integration of all
forms of liberation. On his headstone is a haiku that he himself wrote:

> The spring that here flows,
> That flows so abundantly,
> I bless, I bless it.

The testimony of Father Oshida allows us to add two important refinements to what we have already said about intrareligious dialogue.

An important feature of his life, which is also found in other
Asian protagonists of dialogue, is the way he situates dialogue within all that is required for life in society. Unlike the
pioneers from the West who were mostly concerned about
spirituality, Fathers Aloysius Pieris, Michael Amaladoss,
Shigeto Oshida, or Kakishi Kadowaki—much like the Dalai
Lama, Silak Suvaraksa, or Thich Nhat Hanh—never separate

[2] "Ce que j'entends par 'Zen'," in *Les Voies de l'Orient* 35 (April 1990): 3.

interreligious dialogue from the commitment to justice, concern for the poor, and respect for nature. They remind us that the encounter of religions is not a matter for specialists. It can never be an isolated task; it cannot stand on its own, not in Asia, not in Africa—not in the West.

Another important feature of the spiritual journey of Father Oshida is that it illustrates very clearly the three stages of interreligious encounter. He was introduced to Buddhism as a child but at some point, not finding what he needed, discovered Christianity and rejected Buddhism. Later, however, he became reconciled with most of his original tradition. Those who make this kind of pilgrimage today are numerous. Initially they live, more or less explicitly, in the tradition—for example, the Christian tradition—they received from their upbringing. Then comes the encounter with another spiritual tradition, a discovery that is often experienced as a new conversion, or at least access to a new and decisive dimension. There follows a third stage, at which, without denying the second, it becomes possible to return to their original tradition, now purified. Arrival at this third stage seems to me the mark of interreligious encounter at the deepest level. Until this passing over and coming back is experienced, one cannot really talk about dialogue; it is still a conversion, which involves a renunciation of or rupture with one's first affiliation. Dialogue is only possible when genuine contact between the two traditions is restored. In this perspective, one could therefore define intrareligious dialogue as "a continuous internal confrontation, a give-and-take between two traditions that are being lived out."

It should be noted again that this third stage is not a synthesis, a harmonious coming together of the first two. If that were the case, we would have a new entity that would render obsolete the first two steps. The point of dialogue is not to remove or overcome differences; it looks for ways to maintain the "force field" created by the two sides of the encounter.

In certain circumstances a synthesis may nevertheless be useful. I am thinking here of Karlfried Graf Dürckheim who did a great service to the West by proposing a synthesis between the Christian tradition of the West and the Buddhist tradition of the East. In his many books and very impressive personal contacts, he communicated to many Europeans the treasures of Eastern wisdom, which he related to the heart of the Christian tradition. However, the teaching he proposes is the result of his own efforts at synthesis. What he has done goes beyond dialogue. It spares those who follow him from having to go through the effort of encountering otherness. There is a logic to his approach since, in his Institute for Initiatic Therapy at Todtmoos-Rütte, the work of encountering oneself and all that is strange therein is a goal that is already challenging enough for those who go there.

However, others are called to take the path of dialogue, to be constantly exposed to new questions. In this case, the give and take is never resolved; internal dialogue is ongoing and constantly raises new questions. In fact, when we come face-to-face with another tradition, we discover wonderful similarities but also troubling inconsistencies. The way of dialogue as it was lived at Takamori, and as some Christians are striving to follow, can be a source of strength, but it is often a source of great uncertainty . To avoid dead ends and wasted time on this path, which is always a bit precarious, certain guideposts are necessary. Fortunately there are already a good number of books that can help. [3]

---

[3] Michael L. Fitzgerald and John Borelli, *Interfaith Dialogue: A Catholic View* (Maryknoll, NY: Orbis Books, 2006); Notto R. Thelle, *Who Can Stop the Wind? Travels in the Borderland between East and West* (Collegeville, MN: Liturgical Press, 2010); William Skudlarek, ed., *The Attentive Voice: Reflections on the Meaning and Practice of Interreligious Dialogue* (Brooklyn, NY: Lantern Books, 2011); Robert Magliola, *Facing Up to Real Doctrinal Difference: How Some Thought-Motifs from Derrida Can Nourish the*

A *Lectio Divina* of Other Religions

Among the many good ways to embark on the path of dialogue, I will concentrate on the monastic way since it is one I am more familiar with. The traditional monastic method of reading the Bible, called *lectio divina*, is about discerning the Word of God in the holy text and accepting what one has discerned. There are different approaches to the Bible: historical, philosophical, literary, or psychological. The most accurate reading, however, is the one that strives to hear the call that God addresses to us through these texts, because ultimately we believe that they are inspired by the Holy Spirit.

This practice of spiritual discernment is actually an interiorized form of hospitality. The method of *lectio divina* brings to a venerable text, biblical or other, the respect due to a stranger, knowing that this stranger is also a messenger of God. Could we not, therefore, adopt this method to read the spiritual testimony of the followers of other religions? It is certainly the way Father Le Saux read the Upanishads or Christian de Chergé the Qur'an side-by-side with the Bible.

It should be noted that the encounter is not limited to texts, as the word *lectio* would suggest. Art can also be a great introduction. Images, rituals, and sacred places are expressions of spirituality that we are invited to "read." In them there will be a great amount of history, literature, politics, culture, and also content that is less edifying—as is also the case with the Bible—but by respectfully welcoming these testimonies, we can discover hidden treasures.

To be faced with spiritual traditions that are unfamiliar does not, therefore, put us in an unfavorable position. In our

---

Catholic-Buddhist Encounter (Kettering, OH: Angelico Press, 2014); James L. Fredericks and Tracy Sayuki Tiemeier, eds., *Interreligious Friendship after* Nostra ætate (New York: Palgrave Macmillan, 2015).

own Christian tradition we have a method that can help those who are resolutely engaged in intrareligious dialogue. Three stages can be distinguished.

Lectio divina requires that right from the beginning of our encounter we listen respectfully. Offering hospitality means that we first of all make sure our home is ready to receive our guests. The second step is to read the sacred text very objectively and ponder it. This means that we recognize the unalterable otherness of the guest who enters our home. But we must go further so that, as in the prayer and contemplation to which *lectio* leads us, interreligious encounter may culminate in communion and the expectation of a "blessing" from our guest.

Preparing a Welcoming Dwelling

Thomas Merton specified the requirements of such a dialogue in a lecture he prepared for a conference that was held in Kolkata:

> This contemplative dialogue must be reserved for those who have been seriously disciplined by years of silence and by long habit of meditation. I would add that it must be reserved for those who have entered with full seriousness into their own monastic tradition and are in authentic contact with the past of their own religious community.[4]

The point could not be made more explicitly: Tourists keep out!

When welcoming people from another religion, the first thing to do is ensure that they will be received in a place that is pleasing. We need to remember that we are welcoming them to our home. Interreligious encounter is more than "faith to faith." If that were the case, we could content ourselves with sticking to doctrinal formulations. Interreligious encounter is

---

[4] *The Asian Journal of Thomas Merton*, 316.

"fidelity to fidelity," that is to say, a meeting at the level of a faith that is lived, reflected on, and perhaps at times endured. It is therefore essential that those who choose this path of intrareligious encounter have acquired a genuine spiritual maturity and great freedom. Whether they be monks in the strict sense or not, they must have learned to persist in silence before the Mystery, to endure uncertainty and emptiness. In short, they must have created a welcoming space within themselves. Only then, as we have seen with the pioneers of the dialogue, will they be able to welcome the testimony of another tradition into their spiritual home, be deeply moved by it, and consent to be changed by this encounter without fear of losing their faith. They will exclaim with Saint John of the Cross, "Well and good if all things change, Lord God, provided we are rooted in you."[5]

However, this requirement should not be too rigid lest deeper dialogue be put off indefinitely. Resolutely setting out on this way can be a way of helping faith to grow. If there is only a tiny flame in the fireplace, too much draft will blow it out, but if the flame is strong, opening the draft will make it even stronger. Once we gain some confidence, we must move forward boldly. Let us recall the exhortation of King Ashoka, an Indian emperor of the Maurya Dynasty who ruled almost all of the Indian subcontinent from about 268 to 232 BCE: "One should listen to and respect the doctrines professed by others. Beloved-of-the-Gods, King Piyadasi, desires that all should be well-learned in the good doctrines of other religions."[6]

---

[5] *Dichos de luz y amor*, 33. Online at https://thirdordercarmelite.word-press.com/carmelite-feast-days/st-john-of-the-cross-priest-and-doctor/sayings-of-light-and-love-st-john-of-the-cross//.

[6] *The Edicts of King Ashoka*, trans. Ven. S. Dhammika, The Wheel Publication No. 386/387 (Kandy, Sri Lanka, 1993). On Line at DharmaNet: http://www.cs.colostate.edu/~malaiya/ashoka.html.

Welcoming with Respect and Confidence

The requirement of depth must include concern for objective knowledge. *Lectio divina* of the Bible presupposes a prior exegetical approach, otherwise there will be misunderstanding or interpretations that are little more than flights of an overly creative imagination. Similarly, for intrareligious dialogue we must first ensure that the representatives of the traditions we want to encounter are really reliable.[7] The requirement is one of honesty and intellectual integrity.

The ideal is to have a face-to-face meeting with such witnesses—if possible, in the place where they actually live, be that in Asia or in Africa. At the same time, there are now many more opportunities to meet with a spiritual master or other witnesses who are living among us. However, we should not think that meeting with the adherents of other religious traditions is a *sine qua non* for making real contact. I know people who have captured the heart of another tradition simply by reading its sacred texts.

In any case, we should never settle for secondhand information about other religions. It is true that most books on the market spare us the trouble of having to interpret the sources and already offer us syntheses. Here again we have the situation I mentioned when speaking of Dürckheim. Nonetheless, those who are really serious about wanting to get to the heart of another spiritual tradition cannot be dispensed from going to the sources. Nothing can replace access to original texts, even though most of us will have to read them in translation. What would we think of a Buddhist who claims to know Christianity but has never read the New Testament? We

---

[7] Some Christians have not taken this precaution and have gone astray in sects; they then concluded that any contact with the East was dangerous. See Joseph-Marie Verlinde, *L'expérience interdite* (Versailles: Saint Paul, 1999).

should further note that this approach is not only for scholars who have the time to devote to such study. Great texts like the Bhagavad Gita, the Tao Te Ching, the Dhammapada, or the Qur'an are not that hard to come by. But we must make the effort, take the time, and seek help.

Sacred texts are, however, not the only means of access to the heart of religions. Some practices are very privileged paths. When we can embrace a spiritual path, like Hatha Yoga, *vipassanā*, or Zen, or some artistic path developed in these settings, such as the "tea ceremony," we carry in our bodies and in our whole person a spiritual tradition that transforms us.

Such a confident acceptance does not leave us unscathed. That is part of the experience of hospitality. When we welcome a guest into our home, we put ourselves under his or her influence. But we need not fear any and all transformations. There are certainly changes that disfigure and distort, but others, on the contrary, reinforce and reveal our true nature. To illustrate this, I like to use the example of a potter and a kiln. The potter's role is to mold a vase, a bowl, a jug. For this he chooses the clay and shapes it. He allows it to dry and then gently puts it into the kiln when it is still dull and brittle. The piece that comes out of the kiln after the firing is much like the one he had put in, but it is not the same! It has the same shape and not one ounce of clay has been added, but it is very different. It is now more solid, has acquired a new color, and has even became sonorous. The fire has mightily enhanced the work of the potter.

This is only an image, but it illustrates that change can be beneficial and even revelatory. All the possibilities of the completed work were already contained in the molded piece, but without the fire, its true nature had not yet been revealed. There are, therefore, changes that are revelatory and even constitutive. That is something we constantly experience through major interpersonal encounters. They can be decisive for the formation of our person. Similarly, in the spiritual life, we can see that without such an encounter, without receiving the radiance of a witness from elsewhere, Christian or not, faith is likely to remain dull and brittle.

Finally, if welcoming is to be really respectful and confident, we need to ensure that it move on to the final stage, the hope of blessing.

Hoping for a Blessing

The demands of an authentic encounter may indeed seem difficult if they are not animated by strong motivation. Moreover, the fruitfulness of interreligious encounter and the energy to engage in it depend on the purity of the intentions that motivate it and on our expectations. It is therefore always necessary to ask ourselves about our motives for encountering others.

We must recognize that the more or less conscious motivation that leads people to intercultural or interspiritual encounter is often tinged with a desire for some benefit, even if that benefit be spiritual. But this kind of quest darkens and eventually distorts encounter.

Prior to the mid-twentieth century, before we imagined the possibility of a real exchange, we did not hesitate to lay hold of the riches, including the spiritual riches, of nations, even— as was said about Hatha Yoga—"to extract these treasures from their pagan dross." We still hold on to this mentality when we look for some enrichment from our encounters. Enrichment is often the fruit of dialogue, certainly, but it cannot be the goal. We cannot exploit dialogue by considering it as a means to a greater good. Dialogue finds its justification in itself. In any case, intrareligious dialogue has no other purpose than the joy that comes with the discovery of another believer, because at the deepest level, it is an encounter with the Spirit of God, who is always at work in a sincere believer. The purpose of dialogue, therefore, is not peace in the world, as is often said. However—and thanks be to God for it—peace may indeed be the result of dialogue, one of its most precious fruits.

For this reason, the Christian who asks to enter into dialogue with a believer of another religion can in no way require the other to do the same. I sometimes hear people complain about the lack of a positive response to their generous initiatives. But we must remember that the offer we make is like a bottle tossed into the ocean. Out of respect for our dialogue partners, we cannot assume what their reaction will be. Given their history and the current situation of their tradition, their response is unpredictable. Regardless, we continue to offer them our hospitality.

When it comes to negotiating an agreement, we are right to demand reciprocity. If Saudi Arabia is allowed to build a mosque in Rome, it is right to ask for approval to build a church in Riyadh. Intrareligious dialogue, however, since it takes place at the spiritual level, should always be unconditional and free. At Takamori Father Oshida used to say, "We should not choose the people who can come to us. If we choose, we choose ourselves. Receive each one as a mystery of Christ."[8] In doing so, we are in accord with the spirit of Jesus who proposed that the feast be open to all who come. "You will be blessed, because they cannot repay you" (Luke 14:14).

This is why we can still go one step further. We can transform our motives so they are more in harmony with the Gospel. While demanding nothing, we hope for everything from our dialogue partner. It may seem paradoxical to ask for nothing and expect everything, but such is the dynamic of authentic encounter. In the chapter of his Rule on the reception of guests (RB 53), St. Benedict asks the abbot of the monastery to perform the ancient rite of washing the feet of the

[8] *Enseignements de Vincent Oshida*, 10.

visitors, and he adds that during this time the community is to sing a verse from the Psalms, "We ponder your steadfast love, O God, in the midst of your temple" (Ps 48:9). The visit of a stranger is indeed a blessing, a manifestation of God's mercy.

Acceptance of the other is more than just waiting, more than a simple availability. To accommodate guests, one goes out to meet them, hoping to receive something from their presence. If, on the contrary, one expects nothing important, the meeting is reduced to a simple expression of courtesy. Christians for whom self-sufficiency appears to be a beautiful expression of the depth of their faith will find it difficult to think they might receive something of value from believers of other religions. However, a faith that has room for nothing else is a shallow faith. The great witnesses of faith attest that faith is, in fact, an experience of unknowing and infinite questioning. The encounter with other believers is grounded in such a faith, a faith driven by hope. The purpose of the encounter with other believers is not to put an end to this questioning, but to revive it, thanks to the way we are aroused by their way of believing, even when it is incompatible with ours. All true interreligious meeting is lived in this eschatological perspective. Christian de Chergé is a privileged witness of that infinite quest. One could describe his entire approach as a theology of hope.[9]

Evangelical Universalism

Throughout this brief study, I have kept in mind this fundamental question: Does interreligious encounter endanger the faith of those who are deeply involved in it? Do people

---

[9] Christian Salenson, *Christian de Chergé: A Theology of Hope*, Cistercian Studies 247 (Collegeville, MN: Liturgical Press, 2012).

who concentrate on developing the evangelical requirement of hospitality risk neglecting other requirements of their Christian belonging? Doesn't being immersed, as it were, in a sea of religions inevitably relativize or distort one's faith?

We have seen that all the pioneers who, even before the council, followed their vocation to enter into dialogue changed dramatically throughout their lives, to the point that they were almost unrecognizable in the end. Their choices and their findings leave many questions unanswered. We can understand that people are perplexed when they see how much those who were deeply engaged in interreligious encounters changed, at least in terms of their appearance.

Rather than being alarmed at the risk of too much openness, we have looked favorably, and often with admiration, on these witnesses to the vitality of the Gospel. Now to be even more clear about the conversion to the Gospel that is demanded by the current situation, we must also consider the opposite risk, that of being closed in on oneself. What happens when fear isolates believers and deprives them of any involvement with others? We know that throughout the centuries churches have often given in to this temptation. There is no need to revisit that history. However, it is obvious that such a defensive attitude, one that is concerned above all to preserve the treasure of the faith, is still present in some Christian circles and, to a certain degree, in each one of us.

Let us consider how this attitude manifests itself and how Jesus responded. Already in the Hebrew Scriptures, certain of the later books show that the temptation to insularity is ever present. We see that the option of isolation and rejection of others was adopted by the people of Israel on their return from exile in Babylon. After having known a period of glory and having seen all nations and all their wealth converging on Jerusalem, the situation was reversed and the holy city was no longer the object of its neighbors' envy. In order to protect the nation as much as possible against all risks of contamination by foreigners, the attitude of the leaders of the people then became fiercely defensive and xenophobic.

When we look at the texts of the gospels, we find that Jesus deliberately reacted against this attitude. He begins by denouncing the compulsion to defend at all costs the integrity of one's tradition against outside influence. There are numerous discussions about the laws of purity in the gospels. Jesus is regularly attacked and accused of violating the Sabbath or of not observing a particular rule regarding food or ritual purity. He is also accused of questioning the importance of the temple. These charges are not marginal; the issue of purity is central to the Gospel. It even seems that Jesus' opposition to certain Jewish practices was the major cause of his condemnation by the clerical caste. By challenging these traditions regarding ritual purity, he questioned the identity of the Israelites and thus their very existence. One can well understand why the officials intervened: "It is better for you to have one man die for the people than to have the whole nation destroyed" (John 11:50).

Christ goes on the attack against those who advocate a defensive and exclusive purity, who propose the elimination of any foreign influence as a way to preserve Jewish identity. Allow me to quote at length the observation of Daniel Marguerat:

> Jesus passes from a defensive to an *active* understanding of purity. The other is not a threat but an opportunity. Relationship with others is no longer stigmatized as a potential risk of pollution but as the locus where believers are invited to fulfil their purity. We can understand why the Nazarene's participation in communal meals, his shocking relationships, and his healings played such an important role in his activities. By going against the established order and associating with the outcasts of his time, Jesus was paradoxically demonstrating his own purity.[10]

[10] Daniel Marguerat and Eric Junod, *Qui a fondé le christianisme?* (Paris: Bayard, Labor et Fides, 2010), 33.

Placed in an interfaith context, this way of understanding Jesus' position opens up broad perspectives. The welcoming of other believers is not necessarily a danger; it can even be an opportunity finally to give concrete expression to the universalism of the Gospel, the very point we have been making throughout this study.

One of the most valuable fruits of the encounter of religions is the rediscovery of this central intuition of Jesus: unconditional openness.

Here too, however, as in the case of evangelical hospitality in interreligious encounter, we must not be naive about implementing the intuition of Christ in the interreligious setting of the present time. Obviously, Jesus was not thinking about interreligious dialogue! At that time, in that part of the world, that would have been unimaginable. The resolute openness he proclaimed has to be seen within the limits of the place where he lived.

Nevertheless, in that context and within those limitations, he welcomed foreigners, including the centurion at Capernaum and the Syro-Phoenician woman in the country of Tyre. Expressing his admiration for the faith of these foreigners, he opened up new perspectives. What he said of the Ninevites or the Queen of Sheba already clearly indicates his desire to do away with legalistic strictures. He respectfully observed the fundamental requirements of the Law and of worship, but his focus on the essentials kept him free. Also, in certain situations, he invited his disciples to go further than they could imagine and to surpass expressions of faith and prayer that were conventional and restrictive. He recalls that "you will worship the Father neither on this mountain nor in Jerusalem. . . . The hour is coming, and is now here, when the true worshipers will worship the Father in spirit and truth" (John 4:21, 23).

The evangelists carefully recorded these gestures and these words, because the first Christian communities seem to have had difficulties in implementing the requirements they implied.

The book of Acts was specifically written to proclaim the mystery of Jesus in this universalist perspective. This intention is evident, from the story of Pentecost, which mentions the presence in Jerusalem of "Parthians, Medes, Elamites, and residents of Mesopotamia, Judea and Cappadocia, Pontus and Asia, Phrygia and Pamphylia, Egypt and the parts of Libya belonging to Cyrene, and visitors from Rome, both Jews and proselytes, Cretans and Arabs" (Acts 2:9-11). All these people who converged on Jerusalem that day received the mandate to go and preach the Good News "to all nations, beginning from Jerusalem" (Luke 24:47), as the rest of the book of Acts will indicate. Jerusalem is now not the end point but the starting point. Further on, in chapter ten, there is a detailed description of how Peter ended up going beyond his tribal mentality by his willingness to eat "unclean" foods, accepting the hospitality of the pagan Cornelius, and entering his home. This was how the original Christian community moved toward a genuine universalism. The action and the teaching of Saint Paul were, of course, crucial in this regard because it was he who, without renouncing his origins, made possible the freeing of the Gospel from the provincialism that could have smothered it.

Today the situation of the world and the churches has changed considerably and we can hear the call of the Gospel to welcome the stranger, even those who are strangers in terms of their faith. The point is not to go to the Bible to find arguments to justify this practice but simply to allow ourselves to be inspired by the attitude of Jesus, to look for appropriate ways to respond to the entirely new situation in which we are called to give an account for the hope that is in us.

Paraphrasing a passage from Genesis and with a glint in his eye, Professor Adolphe Gesché used to say, "It is not good for Christians to be alone." It is only in the presence of others that Christians can go beyond a certain confinement that is part of any religion and realize their vocation to witness to the universal benevolence of God the Father, who "makes his sun rise on the evil and on the good, and sends rain on the righteous and on the unrighteous" (Matt 5:45).

Universal acceptance is essential to the Gospel. The invitation to belong to a community of brothers and sisters is always made against this horizon. In the broader context of today's world, the healthy tension between these two movements appears more clearly than ever. It is the task of theologians to explore the right way to harmonize these two components of the Gospel.

As for those who engage in interreligious encounter, they contribute by their paradoxical experience of a radical commitment to the Lord Jesus along with the unconditional acceptance of others in his name. We have seen that the deeper they go in their interreligious encounters, the more courageous they can be. In this way they offer all Christians new ways of living their faith today. But this discovery has only just begun.

.